TRUMP UNIVERSITY

ENTREPRENEURSHIP
101

Books in the Trump University Series

TRUMP
UNIVERSITY

ENTREPRENEURSHIP
1O1

How to Turn Your Idea into
a Money Machine

MICHAEL E. GORDON, PhD

FOREWORD AND CHAPTER 1 BY DONALD TRUMP

John Wiley & Sons, Inc.

ISBN-13: 978-0-470-04712-5

ISBN-10: 0-470-04712-7

Printed in the United States of America.

10   9   8   7   6   5   4   3   2   1

This book is dedicated to the
entrepreneurial spirit within each and every one of us,
striving to burst free.

CONTENTS

CONTENTS

FOREWORD TO THE TRUMP
UNIVERSITY 101 SERIES

People often ask me the secret to my success, and the answer is simple: focus, hard work, and tenacity. I've had some lucky breaks, but luck will only get you so far. You also need business savvy—not necessarily a degree from Wharton, but you do need the desire and discipline to educate yourself. I created Trump University to give motivated businesspeople the skills required to achieve lasting success.

The Trump University 101 Series explains the most powerful and important ideas in business—the same concepts taught in the most respected MBA curriculums and used by the most successful companies in the world, including the Trump Organization. Each book is written by a top professor, author, or entrepreneur whose goal is to help you put these ideas to use in your business right away. If you're not satisfied with the status quo in your career, read this book, pick one key idea, and implement it. I guarantee it will make you money.

DONALD J. TRUMP

ACKNOWLEDGMENTS

Where to begin? I am grateful to so many people: Donald Trump for influencing me to think the boldest entrepreneurial visions; Michael Sexton, president of *Trump University* for his continuous support and willingness to share his entrepreneurial thinking; Richard Narramore, senior editor at Wiley for shaping my thinking and keeping me on track throughout the process; Donald Sexton, author of *Trump University Marketing 101*, for his helpful suggestions; and executives in the Trump Organization who made time available to share their knowledge and experiences—George Ross, Cathy Glosser, E. J. Ridings, and Meredith McIver.

Genuine thanks and appreciation to my business partner and dear friend, Lenard Cohen, for the great odyssey we shared. Without him this book would not have happened.

Particular thanks to: Allan Cohen, Madden Distinguished Professor in Global Leadership at Babson College, for opening this door for me and for his support over many years; Dean Ray Comeau, my friend and colleague at the Harvard University Extension School, for his unflagging motivation and encouragement from beginning to end; Babson Professors Donna Kelley and Andrew Zacharakis for their willingness to review challenging book materials; Richard Luecke for his meticulous, perceptive, and knowledgeable editing support chapter by chapter; Carl Hedberg for his ardent editorial review of the manuscript; Pat Nicolino for being so available to consult with me; Frederick Gillis and Steven Voight for their enthusiastic and tireless research and input on content over many months.

Colleagues and friends: Marianne Abrams, Ian Agranat, Fred Alper, Jim Bath, Candida Brush, Bill Bygrave, Geoffrey Chalmers, Leslie Charm,

ACKNOWLEDGMENTS

Helen Coates, Marcia Cole, Valerie Duffy, Len Green, Bill Johnston, Evelyn Lager, Julian Lange, Louise Lawson, Ed Marram, Jim McKellar, Heidi Neck, Audrey O'Neil, Lyman Opie, Georgia Papavasiliou, Garry Prime, Dean Mark Rice, Elizabeth Riley, Andrea Ross, Joel Shulman, Tom Simon, Steve Spinelli, Randy Stockton, Janet Strimaitis, Natalie Taylor, Jeff Timmons, and Gene Whitman.

And most of all to my family and friends who have empathized and commiserated throughout the birthing of this book: my dear, dear wife and soul mate, Maria, who continuously filled me with confidence, and tolerated book materials strewn around the home; my beloved children, Adam and Deborah; my stepchildren Oscar, Jose, and Elizabeth; my precious sister Sandra; my cherished 98-year-old mother, Jeanne; my niece Andrea's family—Joel, Jake, and Noah; my nephew Stephen's family—Dana, Caleb, and Eli; my cousins Lori, Jerry, and Linda; my wonderful extended family in Mexico—Angelina y toda su familia; friends for life—John Bergman; David and Nancy Weaver; Myron and Marie Waldman; Harold and Eleanor Ottobrini; Jesse and Lora Erlich; Ellis and Debbie Waldman; Lucia, Bruce, Sam, Bianca Santini Fields; and Bev Santini. *Did I leave anyone out? I sincerely hope not!*

Introduction:
Buckle Up for Your
Fantastic Voyage

Let me ask you this before we go further: Why have you picked up this book? I ask because if you are ready and willing, this book will be your guide on an amazing journey. But it is not an easy or risk-free journey! Just as Donald Trump has demonstrated throughout his career, rewards in life are the direct result of imagination, hard work, dedication, and the willingness to take reasoned risks. If creating a business isn't very high on your list of life priorities, this book can do little for you—put it back on the shelf. But if you are like millions of us who derive enormous pleasure from the challenges and rewards of entrepreneurship, then buckle up for your fantastic voyage!

Your voyage is about you and the fulfillment of your life dreams. You are browsing this book for one of the following reasons:

1. You want to learn how to start and grow your own business.
2. You are already in your own business and anxiously want rapid, sustainable, profitable growth.
3. You are currently employed and you have an idea that could become a profitable new division for the company and you want to "champion" this internal venture.
4. You want to reach your full entrepreneurial potential.

These are strong wants inside you; in fact, they are *needs*. You can envision yourself as CEO, president, leader, champion of your own successful venture. And why not?

There is no mystery to entrepreneurship. It is about doing things better, creating value for the customer, and being rewarded for your success. *So what's holding you back?* Some of the common obstacles are lack of start-up capital, the potential for financial loss, career risks, lack of self-confidence, pressure on your family, issues of health and stress, lack of the "Big Idea," minimal tolerance for risk, or being just plain stuck. These concerns are legitimate, and they will be examined at length in Chapter 3 and put into perspective, but *they will not prevent you from realizing your vision.* As your essential guide for your entrepreneurial voyage, this book will help you to move past the roadblocks and onto the racetrack toward your goal.

I am an incurable entrepreneur, several times over, and certainly more to come. My successful ventures include a plastics injection molding company, a static control company that developed and manufactured products for the microelectronics industry, an executive consulting and investment banking firm, a face-to-face business network, a virtual business network connecting entrepreneurs and investors over the Internet, and real estate investing. My experiences in starting and growing these companies will be used throughout this book to highlight the main themes of entrepreneurship that will be of benefit to you. Not all of my ventures were successful, but they surely were not failures. Each nonsuccess was a step in my learning process, taking me to new levels of understanding and confidence, and thereby increasing my chances of succeeding in future attempts.

Success is more than having started and grown businesses. It has to do with what goes on in my mind, my gut, my heart, even my toes (they tingle) when I am following the entrepreneurial scent; the empowerment I feel when my Money Machine takes shape, starts, and grows. And more—the self-confidence and esteem I experience from being my own boss, from having pursued an opportunity, and being rewarded for my dogged persistence; the power of having resources to accomplish whatever I can envision. And still more—being surrounded by the culture I created, a motivated high-power team, satisfied customers and stakeholders. And even more—the afterglow of savoring the process of entrepreneurship and looking forward to the next one.

The start-up phase of my first business was an exhilarating struggle, often intense, sometimes scary, always filled with raw passion. I felt really alive. My mental image was this: I was standing on one side of this terrifying chasm, a bottomless start-up pit where flames of risk were waiting to engulf me. I was like a deer frozen in the headlights—stuck on the wrong side. I could envision myself on the other side, successfully growing my own business. But how to get there?

Well, I crossed that chasm, and my life has been deliciously full because of entrepreneurship. I set a goal for myself to teach entrepreneurship at a prestigious business school as soon as time permitted. I wanted to help eager entrepreneurs in their quest to realize their own entrepreneurial dreams. To my good fortune, 15 years ago I sought and obtained a position as adjunct professor at the preeminent college of entrepreneurship, Babson College. Currently, I am also an adjunct professor at Harvard University Extension School and the International School of Management in Paris. Along the way I have taught at universities and executive education programs in Latin America, Southeast Asia, and Europe. Although I was trained as a chemist, having earned a Bachelor of Science degree from Worcester Polytechnic Institute and a PhD from MIT, my professional life really began when I discovered my twin passions for entrepreneurship and teaching.

This is a guidebook, and it has three objectives: (1) to energize you to take courageous, thoughtful, inexorable steps to your entrepreneurial goal; (2) to demystify the entrepreneurial process from idea through start-up to growth; and (3) to magnify your success as your venture grows. This primer will benefit entrepreneurs-to-be as well as entrepreneurs that are already in their own businesses.

The themes of the book are woven into the Money Machine, an accessible representation of the entrepreneurial process. Your idea/opportunity goes into the top of the machine; the machine processes, refines, and shapes this input; the spigot discharges money. The greater the value you add or create for the customer, the greater will be your profits. Plain and simple: No value, no profits. There are many ways to add customer value, and we will discuss them at length. For now, keep focusing on the essence of adding value for your customer.

During my 25 years as an entrepreneur and 15 years as an educator, I have developed powerful and memorable visual metaphors to communicate entrepreneurial concepts quickly and precisely. "One picture is worth a thousand words." The book employs actual case studies, downloadable worksheets, and war stories from Donald Trump and executives in the Trump Organization. Each chapter concludes with a summary and specific action items that will urge you, even push you, step by exhilarating step, toward your vision.

Shortly after we sold our static control company, my partner, Len and I were in Café Vittorio in the North End of Boston savoring a real Italian cappuccino. Len was reminiscing: "It really is amazing, Mike. We started with an idea, bootstrapped the start-up phase with very limited resources, built a significant business, developed a performance-oriented team, created many new products that became industry standards, sold these products through worldwide distribution, had remarkable profit margins, and sold the company to a public British company." As I pondered his remarks, the image on page xiv crystallized in my mind.

Bigfoot Started with Small Successful Steps

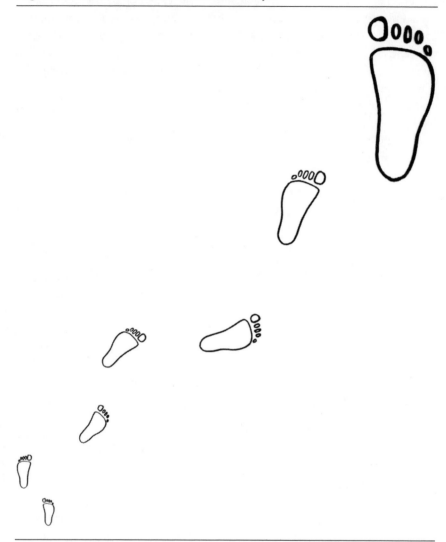

Source: "Bigfoot Started with Small Successful Steps." Copyright © 1992 by Michael E. Gordon.

And that is how you are going to do it: one small successful step after another, each step growing, evolving; each step more certain, more powerful. Are you ready to build your own Money Machine? If you are, this primer will guide you. Buckle up for the most *fantastic* voyage of your life!

Follow your own path because it will bring you to the places you were meant to be.

—Donald J. Trump

The Grand Hyatt Hotel
Photo courtesy of the Trump Organization

1

TRUMP ON

ENTREPRENEURSHIP

by
Donald Trump

Entrepreneurship starts with vision. Without a vision, nothing of consequence will happen. In 1974, I looked at the old Commodore Hotel, next to Grand Central Station in New York City. I did not see a huge, dilapidated, nearly empty building in a seedy neighborhood. I did not see a bankrupt city or the New York real estate market, struggling to survive. I saw a magnificent, first-class convention hotel complex—grandiose, luxurious, and noteworthy. I was a young man of 27, and my vision felt right-sized.

As I made plans to acquire and rebuild the Commodore, I uncovered seemingly insurmountable obstacles. Many people with power had showstopping issues with my plan. The more involved I became, the more daunting were the problems. But I didn't give up. To me, every problem is a well-disguised potential opportunity. Let's face it, if it weren't for these obstacles, that building would have already been snapped up by someone else. Think about that: The obstacles you face also keep out your competitors.

Problems are just the door to success.

Of course there were risks. I am willing to take reasoned risks, but I won't roll the dice. I manage risk so that one nonsuccess does not put me out of the game permanently. The biggest risk in life is the unwillingness to take one.

The rest of the Commodore story is history.[1] It took me five years to pull it off. With financing from the Hyatt Hotel chain, I acquired and rebuilt the property. In 1980, the Grand Hyatt opened—it was a great success from day one. My vision became a reality—and I walked away with $85 million.

I learned a lot about entrepreneurship along the way, especially how to mobilize resources: financial, infrastructure, services of all kinds, and particularly, great talent. You can't do it alone. Building a world-class team is the only way to big success. I called George Ross, one of the great real estate lawyers in New York, and we began to define all the stakeholders we needed to negotiate with. I then brought on the right architectural firm to enable me to communicate my vision. The list of resources was large, and growing: a project manager and team, an investment banking firm, an accounting firm, a marketing firm, administrative support. After carefully selecting my first-class team, I let them run with the ball. But they all knew they were accountable to me to deliver on my initiatives. That's what *The Apprentice* is all about. It is not just another entertaining TV show. It embodies a basic principle of entrepreneurship: Those that can't deliver are not on my team!

You can't do it alone. Building a world-class team is the only way to big success.

In this, and every one of my deals, it was the relationships with key people whose help I needed that made the difference. That's why every entrepreneur needs finely tuned negotiating skills—needs to be tough, yet accommodating at the same time. A win-win result was essential. At the end of each negotiation, I knew that my opponents would turn into my partners. And I wanted to ensure a continuing relationship with them, for this and future deals.

The most important characteristic for any entrepreneur is to be unstoppable. Once in motion, my team and I cannot be stopped. Think of the power of this one word: unstoppable!

Take this from me: Entrepreneurship is not genetic; it can be learned. I make things happen because of my own will, skill, knowledge, and personal power. These are traits you can learn and improve with practice. This is what Trump University and this book are all about.

**Unleash your Entrepreneurial Power.
Refuse to be stopped!**

Michael Gordon is a top entrepreneurship professor and a passionate entrepreneur and consultant. He'll be your mentor and coach. But here's my parting shot: Don't ever give up on yourself before you realize that you can and will "do it." Trust me: A successful business is within your grasp if you really want to make it happen.

2

UNLEASH YOUR
ENTREPRENEURIAL POWER

My father was the cofounder of a meat processing and distribution company, and his concept of training me in the family business was to start me at the bottom. The very bottom! "I want you to learn the business from the ground up," he told me. For starters, Dad put me in charge of the company's hamburger operation. It was a one-person business: *me*. I had a 500-square-foot work area, equipped with a boning bench, a meat grinder, a patty maker, storage shelves, packaging materials, pallets, gloves, telephone, radio, desk, and miscellaneous knives and supplies (no computer in those days). Each morning, I would belly up to the boning bench with knife in hand. I would take a slab of beef, debone the meat, and trim off the fat. The next step was to cram raw chunks into the hopper. Once inside, the meat was chopped between metal grinding blades, and out came raw ground beef. In the second operation, another machine shaped the bulk ground beef into perfect patties that were then packaged by a third machine. The input was chunks of meat plus my labor; the process was mechanical chopping and molding; and the output was packaged ground beef patties. But something really important happened in this simple process: I added value for customers!

If it weren't for my labor and the machines, customers would have to buy the raw beef and chop it themselves, or buy a grinder and form the patties by hand. It doesn't seem like much value, but billions of pounds of ground beef are sold annually in the world. So customers were willing to pay a bit extra for the small value I added.

Since I am producing a product and adding value, does that mean I am an entrepreneur?

Day after boring day, my operation produced ground hamburger patties, amounting to about 200,000 pounds per year. One day I had an idea: What if I produced specialty hamburger patties? I could envision a line of different types and flavors: healthy organic meat from range-fed, steroid-free cows; smoky burgers with bits of smoked bacon added during the grinding operation; Tex-Mex burgers with added salsa and other seasonings; Hawaiian burgers, veggie burgers, turkey burgers . . . (this was in my youth, decades before the existence of prepackaged veggie, healthy, and turkey burgers).

I came up with an idea, and I am thinking how to add unique value. Am I an entrepreneur now?

I actually began to create and eat my prototypes in my spare time. Some of my concoctions were really tasty! Others were unpalatable. Weeks later, when I had developed confidence in my new idea, I asked for a meeting with my father. I brought my successful experiments and a cooking grill to demonstrate my concept. My father sampled the proposed new product line and became enthusiastic.

What happened next was truly exhilarating. For the next two hours, the questions were flying: What kinds of approval do we need from health agencies? How should we price the new product line? Who should we sell to—consumers, distributors, restaurants, supermarkets? Should we sell locally, regionally, nationally, globally? Who will run this business? Should we set this up as a separate business unit and create a branded identity? Do we have competition now or in the future? How can we know if there is an opportunity here? How much money do we need to launch this venture? How much money can the company make in the course of a year? What about other resources—people, space, equipment, infrastructure? The meeting ended on a high note, with my father asking me to write something up about this idea.

(In those days, I knew nothing about the importance of writing a business plan or an executive summary.)

After studying the competition and the potential market, I came to believe that this was a real opportunity to make money. Over the next few weeks I began to write a summary of what needed to be done. My starting point was a detailed list of assumptions, based on questions my father had asked in our meeting. I even calculated our projected financial growth over the next several years. I asked for another meeting and presented my thoughts to my father. He was even more interested. He made a decision to pursue this venture inside the existing company and asked me to run this department, with its own profit and loss accounting.

So here I was at age 17 with the mandate to build a new hamburger business unit inside the meat company.

Since my idea appears to be a real opportunity, and I am to be in charge of this business, am I an entrepreneur now?

Though I faced many challenges, my focus was on getting the new business unit going and making money. My strategy was to create a branded line of hamburger patties (Gordon's Great Gurnseyburgers, Healthy Heiferburgers, Smokey the Bearger, and others) and sell to customers under our brand name, at a premium price. I would sell directly to retail consumers, to distributors, restaurants, and food markets; to everyone except to other meat markets. I knew that if I were successful, competitors would smell the profits and try to horn in on my business. Because I could not prevent that from happening, I would have to rely on my brand recognition to build sales and profits quickly. But I did not want future competitors to see the momentum we were gaining before we were well along with our branding efforts.

Now am I an entrepreneur?

Looking back, I realize that the entrepreneurial spirit was within me, and I was beginning to live the entrepreneurial process. I had developed an idea and, through discussions with more experienced hands, confirmed that it represented a real opportunity for our company. I had even come up with a strategy: to develop a product line of unique hamburgers—burgers that were different from what everyone else was selling. My prototype taste tests were a rudimentary form of market research, and that research told me that customers would value the difference they found in our products. My written summary of the proposed business, including financial projections, brought my idea to a level of practical concreteness.

Was I an entrepreneur at that point? No. I was an almost-entrepreneur: a young man with ideas and plans but with no skin in the game. Like countless other commercial dreamers, I didn't take that bold, risky step of implementing my strategy. I went off to college to pursue my passion for science, and the would-be Great Gordon Burger Empire was forgotten. There was no champion to take up the cause.

Many years would pass before I could truthfully say, "Now, I am an entrepreneur."

ENTREPRENEURSHIP DEFINED

The term *entrepreneurship* leaves much to be desired. You have to wrap your mouth around the word, making creative pronunciation choices on three of the five syllables. Dictionaries define it as the startup and management of a business, with great initiative and risk, for profit. To me, entrepreneurship encompasses these three factors: **M**indset, **A**ctions, **P**rocess:

> **M**indset: Entrepreneurs go through the world continuously seeking ideas and opportunities that can be commercialized. They focus on innovating, doing things better, adding, creating, and *delivering* unique value to customers and to all stakeholders. And they want to be rewarded for their successes. The more value they add, the greater their financial rewards.

> **A**ctions: Entrepreneurs are proactive to the extreme, and once on the opportunity trail, they move mountains to mobilize the necessary resources to accomplish their goals. And then, in the words of Nike, they just "do it," and they do it their own way.

> **P**rocess: Entrepreneurship is a dynamic, continuous, living process.[1] The process is driven by you, the entrepreneur, the founder, the champion. As you build your Money Machine, you will take the following actions:

- Generate *ideas* incessantly.
- Select the real *opportunity* from the heap of ideas.
- Build and empower the *team*.

Figure 2.1   You, Obstacles, Your Goal

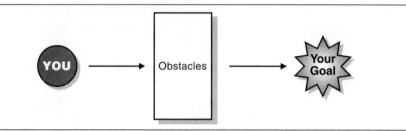

Source: www.CompetitiveSuccess.com, "You, Obstacles, Your Goal." Copyright © 2000 by Michael E. Gordon. Used with permission.

- Mobilize and control necessary *resources*, whether or not you own them.
- Develop an astute *strategy* to capture customers and to generate sales and sustainable profits.
- Develop a compelling *business plan*.
- Assess personal and business *risks*—acceptance/rejection.
- Launch the venture.
- Manage the growing venture.
- Harvest the rewards of success: sell your business, take your business public, or continue to build your venture and pay yourself appropriate and generous compensation.

Feel the entrepreneurial energy and exhilaration in the process: Generate, select, build, mobilize, develop, assess, launch, manage, harvest.

Entrepreneurship is a personal voyage, and your chance of success is greater the more clearly you understand yourself, your goals, and the obstacles you face. In this chapter, we explore you and your goals. The next chapter is devoted to overcoming formidable obstacles. Figure 2.1 depicts this framework.

YOU

YOU are at the top of the entrepreneurial process. There is no such thing as an entrepreneurial process without you, the committed, passionate, unstoppable entrepreneur. You make everything happen, and that's what is really exciting. You won't do it alone; you will find the opportunity, build your team, mobilize the necessary resources, define the vision, and act boldly. And you are completely free to do it your own way. To learn the rules—and then break them. Don't burden yourself with the wrong question: *Am I an entrepreneur?* Having coached thousands of students of entrepreneurship at all levels—PhD, MBA, executive education, college and high school—over a 15-year period, I can promise that you are not alone with this anxiety. This is a very common concern for entrepreneurs-to-be, but frankly it is the wrong question, and the question itself leads to inaction. Entrepreneurship is not a yes/no phenomenon: Yes I am an entrepreneur, No I am not an entrepreneur. Entrepreneurship is not genetic. It has nothing to do with your chromosomes or inherited traits. Entrepreneurs are not born; they make things happen because of their own will and skill and knowledge. And these traits can be learned and enhanced.

Concentrate on the right question: *How can I learn what I need to know and improve my entrepreneurial skills to maximize my chance of succeeding?* Successful entrepreneurs have developed personal power skills, which can be learned and strengthened. Further on in this chapter, we crawl through a checklist of your own Essential Entrepreneurial Power Skills and ways to enhance them. Don't ever give up on yourself before you realize that you can and will do it. Trust me: It is within your grasp if you really *want* to make it happen.

YOUR GOAL

It's easy to get confused in life. You want so many things that you lose focus. There is nothing wrong with having a full palette of goals—it is a reflection of your human passions, needs, motivators, personal driving forces. Without strong goals, not much would be accomplished in life. The fact is that successful entrepreneurs have the tenacity of a hound dog on the scent of *one* rabbit. A hound dog following more than one scent will always come up empty. The one goal we are pursuing in this book is the start-up and growth of your business.

Suggestion: Pause here; mark this page and create a list of your life goals, in order of priority. Be inclusive. List all of your goals in all categories—business, social, personal, athletic, spiritual, artistic, and so on. Now go through the list and cross out all but the top three. *If starting and growing your own business is not one of your top three goals in life, this book will be of limited benefit.* If you are uncertain, please keep reading. If your own business *is* in your top three goals, move forward, full speed ahead. But recognize that other goals will need to be put on the back burner to maximize your chance of success. Let the power of commitment and focus lead you forward.

"Whatever you can do, or dream you can do, begin it. Boldness has genius, power, and magic in it. Begin it NOW!"—Goethe

---

When it comes to advice, I am better at giving than receiving. However, I did follow my own advice this time and created my extensive goal list. I asked myself: What is the one goal inside me that is ready for expression now? And the answer was . . . writing this book. Think of the power of committing to my one most important goal. As soon as I developed that clarity, doors opened for me. My energy went sky high; my mind went into high gear; my creative juices began flowing. I was on a roll. Within two hours, I had the table of contents on paper, my office became a war room, and I began assembling piles of my teaching materials to follow the table of contents. I then went to the library to study the competition and to look for untapped market niches to position the book properly. I compiled a list of questions and resource needs: Who was my target audience? What kind of help do I need? When can I get to market? I created a Milestone Chart and taped it to the wall over my computer so that it would always be staring back at me, demandingly, unforgivingly, dispassionately. I developed a To-Do List along with my Keys to Success (this powerful concept will be discussed in Chapter 19) and taped them to my wall. By the end of the day, I felt the power of my commitment to succeed. I couldn't sleep one wink that night. Graciously, my wife listened to my excitement into the wee hours of the morning.

ESSENTIAL ENTREPRENEURIAL POWER SKILLS

Earlier in this chapter, I asserted that entrepreneurship is not genetic: It can be learned. Successful entrepreneurs like Donald Trump have acquired skills, knowledge, and experiences to make their bold visions happen. Let's look at the framework of learnable skills. There are 11 Essential Entrepreneurial Power Skills that you need in your toolbox to empower you and maximize your chance of success in any endeavor, not just entrepreneurship:

1. *Assess the present situation accurately.* The first Entrepreneurial Power Skill is to hone your ability to observe, collect information, and understand the situation facing you and your company. What

is going on in the world around you—internally and externally? Your competition, customers, team, resource requirements, technology, industry dynamics, *everything* you need to know to make astute, objective decisions. If you begin with the wrong assumptions, you will invariably get the wrong answers.

2. *Go after bold visions.* Having gone through the assessment, you are in a position to establish clear, measurable goals. But make them bold! You are capable of accomplishing considerably more than you realize. Let me share with you one of the most important concepts in this book:

The Power of Zero

Let's say your vision is to build a company that will grow to $500,000 in sales in five years. Now start adding zeros. Ask yourself: *How* can I grow my company to $5 million? What must I think and do differently? Add another zero. How can I grow my company to $50 million? Do you notice the power of zero and the word *How?* Your mind refocuses on how to accomplish the boldest vision. (Refer to Chapter 20 for further discussion.)

3. *Be unstoppable.* The successful completion of every project requires your meticulous attention to detail and the refusal to let milestones slip by. Start with the mind-set that you and your team cannot be stopped. Facing any obstacle, large or small, you will go over, under, around, through—and you will be unstoppable. Can you feel the power of this simple idea—refusal to be stopped? Just show up and get it done.

4. *Negotiate firmly and "win-winly."* Every interaction between people can benefit from proficiency at win-win negotiation. In the book *Getting to Yes*,[2] the authors develop the four principles required to build continuing relationships through negotiation: (a) Separate the people from the problem; (b) focus on interests, not positions; (c) invent options for mutual gain; and (d) insist on objective criteria. The challenge is to accomplish what you want while retaining an abundant relationship. Win-win negotiating skills have been so important to me that I have included an entire chapter on this topic (Chapter 16).

5. *Solve problems.* There is rarely a day in my business or personal life that a problem doesn't crop up that needs to be resolved. Things are going along fine, and suddenly—a problem. Kepner and Tregoe[3] have developed a systematic seven-step approach to solving

problems: (a) Identify the deviation, (b) specify the deviation, (c) define the boundaries, (d) examine the distinctions, (e) look for changes, (f) test for cause, and (g) verify the cause. The point is that there is a process you can learn and apply to systematically solve problems. You don't have to wing it.

6. *Make good decisions.* The ability to make good decisions is essential to success in business and personal life. Bad decisions lead to nonsuccess. So, how can you enhance your decision-making skills? Kepner and Tregoe have also developed a systematic approach to making decisions: (a) Setting out the decision statement, (b) specifying the ideal, (c) classifying and weighing the criteria, (d) stating the alternatives, (e) evaluating the alternatives, (f) projecting future consequences, and (g) making the choice. I use the Kepner and Tregoe processes frequently, and my decision-making ability continues to improve.

7. *Brainstorm.* Brainstorming is the process of harnessing the thinking, experiences, and imagination of a group to generate creative ideas and to solve problems. The collective knowledge of a group is vastly greater than that of any one individual, and this is the power of the brainstorming process. This skill will be discussed in some detail in Chapter 3.

8. *Mobilize powerful resources.* It is not possible to accomplish anything of consequence without understanding the importance of leveraging resources. Entrepreneurial resources can be thought of as *anything* (absolutely anything) that moves your venture further and faster—with least risk. This subject will be discussed in detail in Chapter 14.

9. *Communicate effectively.* Let's take inventory. You have assessed the situation, put your bold vision in place, and established performance initiatives. Now what happens? Nothing—unless you communicate consistently and constantly to all stakeholders who need to be informed. Let there be no confusion in any stakeholder's mind about what you expect to accomplish. It is not possible to influence anyone without effective, charismatic communication abilities. And in case you are wondering, charismatic communication *can* be learned and enhanced with practice. (www.andybounds.com)

10. *Act decisively.* Entrepreneurship is a contact sport. It is not only about thinking, planning, coordinating, and visioning. IT IS ABOUT DOING: Figuring out how to get the task done and being unstoppable in its execution.

11. *Behave with integrity.* There are people for whom you would do anything and others with whom you would not waste your time. The

difference is the quality of the person's character and behavior. Good citizens attract the most beneficial karma. I am referring to the following traits and behaviors: ethics, honesty, trustworthiness, reliability, fairness, maturity, professionalism, humor, delivers on promises, is knowledgeable, shows up on time (even early), has a balanced perspective, is a win-win player, has good listening skills, good leading skills, and good following skills.

As you look over these 11 Essential Entrepreneurial Power Skills, note two things: They are certainly not genetic and they can be learned and enhanced. How strong are your Essential Entrepreneurial Power Skills? Take the self-diagnostic test in Exhibit 2.1 to find out. Then think about what you can do to strengthen areas of weakness. Use every opportunity to practice.

SUMMARY

Entrepreneurs go through the world seeking opportunities to commercialize. They innovate to bring value to the customer and to all stakeholders. The greater and more unique the value, the greater are their profits. Entrepreneurs are proactive to the extreme, and it is this action orientation that leads to their successes in business and in life. The power of commitment and focus can make you unstoppable. The Essential Entrepreneurial Skills are like muscles: They strengthen with practice.

Actions

√ Constantly practice the 11 Essential Entrepreneurial Power Skills.
√ Create a war room: Set up your office area with a file cabinet and enough wall space for Milestone Charts, To-Do Lists, Resource Needs, Keys to Success, and Critical Risks (these will be defined in Chapter 19).
√ Set your expectations: Don't presume that it will be easy; but the exhilaration and life-changing results will be more than worth the extensive effort and hard work.
√ Do not spend any significant money until you have read the entire book, and particularly Chapter 7.

Pep Talk

You want to do it. You can do it. You will do it. You are unstoppable!

Downloadable Exhibit 2.1   Essential Entrepreneurial Power Skills*

Power Skills	Self-Assessment Least Best 1 2 3 4 5	Action to Improve
Assess the present situation accurately		
Go after bold visions		
Be unstoppable		
Negotiate firmly and "win-winly"		
Solve problems		
Make good decisions		
Brainstorm		
Mobilize powerful resources		
Communicate effectively		
Act decisively		
Behave with integrity (Ethics, honesty, trustworthiness, reliability, fairness, maturity, professionalism, humor, delivers on promises, is knowledgeable, shows up on time [even early], has a balanced perspective, is a win-win player, has good listening skills, good leading skills, good following skills, and so on)		

Source: www.CompetitiveSuccess.com, "Essential Entrepreneurial Power Skills." Copyright © 2000 by Michael E. Gordon. Used with permission. ***A blank version of this page can be downloaded from www.trumpuniversity.com/entrepreneurship101 for your personal use.***

3

FEEL THE FEAR—
DO IT ANYWAY

What is preventing you from growing your own business? Our objectives in this chapter are to understand the seemingly impenetrable obstacles that are blocking you, to develop an action plan, and to move beyond these obstacles. If this were easy, there would be many, many more entrepreneurs. After all, why not be in business for yourself, if you so choose? But the fact is, there are many frustrated "wannabe" entrepreneurs. If you can sail beyond these obstacles, you will be well on your way to becoming an "alreadybe."

Let's reformat the diagram (Figure 2.1) from the previous chapter, and concentrate on Figure 3.1. You are pursuing your one, and only one, entrepreneurial opportunity. There are potholes, barricades, moats, hardships, and challenges of all kinds all along the path (otherwise it would be boring). Your concerns may be financial or emotional, related to time, fear, self-doubt, career, family, health, lack of knowledge, inertia, risk, being just plain stuck, or lacking the Big Idea. It doesn't matter. You will not be stopped. You will go over, under, around, or through each barrier. How will that happen? You will reach each milestone and goal with the help of this book and with your increasing entrepreneurial power. Note in

Figure 3.1   Under, Over, Around, Through Obstacles

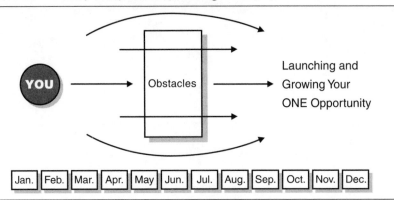

Figure 3.1 that the dimension of time has been added, along with arrows of focus. Do not let milestones slip for any reason. There are always excuses for why things don't get done on time. The most successful people in life are like supertankers: steady, strong, unstoppable.

OBSTACLES

You know deep down why you want to be in business for yourself: creating value from practically nothing, pursuing your life passion, the possibilities of great wealth and living large, being your own boss, being rewarded for your successes, feeling alive, feeling successful, feeling the warmth of self-esteem, being in the center of the Money Machine that you created, having resources to pursue your life vision, controlling the most precious asset you have—your time. But there are real and perceived obstacles and risks. Your task is to figure out ways to get over, under, around, and through these obstacles. It can be done, and in fact it is done every year by about 750,000 entrepreneurs. Next year, the number will be at least 750,001, including you.

The first thing to remember is that entrepreneurship is a trial-and-error activity, as illustrated in Figure 3.2: The Trying Game. Each arrow represents an attempted startup of a new venture. The more times you try, the more you learn, the better you get at rebounding. My own track record includes 11 attempted startups, but only six resulted in businesses that had

Figure 3.2   The Trying Game

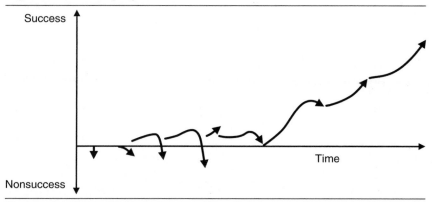

Source: www.CompetitiveSuccess.com, "The Trying Game." Copyright © 1992 by Michael E. Gordon. Used with permission.

operating profits, and to varying degrees. The plan, then, is to control all risks so that nonsuccess in the pursuit of one opportunity does not create irreparable harm to you. Remember that nonsuccess is not a failure unless it puts you out of the game permanently. To illustrate my point, try this: When you come across successful entrepreneurs at cocktail parties, at your health club, at networking meetings, at other business and social events, ask them about their entrepreneurial histories. You will hear repeatedly that most of them (perhaps all) did not succeed on their first attempt. They kept going, repositioning the first opportunity or abandoning it to explore another one. That was my situation; the nonsuccesses strengthened me, they did not weaken me.

The classic vignette about Thomas Edison epitomizes this point: Thomas Edison, the greatest inventor of all time (1,093 patents: phonograph, stock ticker machine, medical X-ray devices, carbon telephone transmitter, etc.), was aggressively attempting to develop a filament for the electric light bulb. He and his team conducted more than 8,000 experiments, trying every conceivable candidate—silk, carbon, metal, thread, ceramic, composites, and so on—under every imaginable atmosphere, in vacuum, nitrogen, argon, in all possible configurations, thicknesses, amperages, voltages. At one point, an acquaintance asked him, "Mr. Edison, how can you keep going in the face of 8,000 failures? Why aren't you crushed by the futility and frustration?" Edison replied, "I never had one failure. I learned from every attempt, and each experiment led me to more likely pathways, and I will eventually succeed." Lights on!

What follows are the most common obstacles. Which ones are holding you back?

Obstacle 1. *Lack of Financial Resources*

You can soften this obstacle immediately by encircling it with action-oriented questions. For example: Where should you look for start-up capital? How can you proceed so that money does not stop or limit you? What do you have to do to move forward with your limited financial resources? In fact, all obstacles should be encircled with questions that become calls to action, rather than showstoppers. You will need money to launch and grow your venture. The issue is how much. If you have a compelling opportunity, I can assure you that you will get the money you need. Further on in this chapter, there is an example of a brainstorming session to move you beyond the money obstacle. Also, Chapter 17 is devoted entirely to raising money.

Obstacle 2. *Potential for Financial Loss*

To give you a sense of perspective, keep the Trying Game in mind. You are beginning to invest in what you believe is an opportunity. If your venture does not make it, the next time you attempt a start-up, you will be more savvy and your chances of succeeding will be greater. Don't make major expenditures until you have a strong sense that you are on the scent of a real opportunity. Specifically, what amounts of financial loss are you worried about?

The graph in Figure 3.3 presents all possible scenarios for the early stages of every business. Look at the points in parentheses: (1) Development Stage, where you are spending money to develop your product or service for commercialization; (2) Zero Stage, the point beyond which you have just received your first dollar of sales from your first customer; Point (3) Nonsuccess at some time before reaching Breakeven Sales; and Point (4) Breakeven Sales, the point at which your incoming sales just cover your outflowing costs.

Note that there are only two points of potential loss: Point (1): You could lose all Development Stage expenditures that you made before you launch your business. This is called the sunk costs to develop your product or service and to ready it for market. Point (3): If your business does not make it after launch, you would lose additional money from cash

Figure 3.3   Growth Stages and Points of Financial Loss

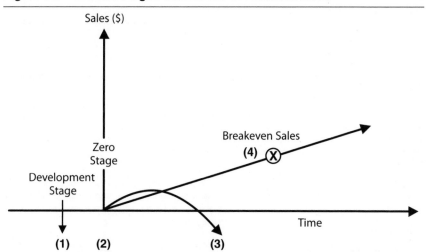

Source: www.CompetitiveSuccess.com, "Growth Stages and Points of Financial Loss."
Copyright © 1996 by Michael E. Gordon. Used with permission.

flowing out of your business faster than cash flowing into your business. If you reach point (4) Breakeven Sales, you have succeeded. Onward and upward!

Exhibit 3.1 focuses your attention on these two critical points of loss. Your task is to define as closely as possible how much money you will need, and might lose, at each of the two Points, (1) and (3).

These are your two concerns: At what point might your business not make it, and how much money in total will you lose in the worst case? These are not pleasant thoughts, but isn't it comforting to be in control of this important money issue? Then the obstacle doesn't appear to be un-manageable. If the total amount of loss through Points (1) and (3) is af-fordable, recoverable, and not threatening, you can make the decision to take the first step. Consider it the cost of education. You can pull the plug at any time. *BUT you just might begin to succeed!*

> **Once you know how much money you are worried about, you can then figure out how worried to be.**

Are we talking about a life-threatening amount, or a sum that you would be willing to risk to explore a chance of a lifetime? This depends on your particular financial situation. The short answer is: Don't put the

Downloadable Exhibit 3.1 Stages of Financial Needs and Potential Losses*

Stages of Financial Need	Projected Financial Needs and Potential Losses
Development Stage **(1)** Concept and prototype development, proof of customer demand, business plan development, people resources, readying your product/service for market, others	Estimate your financial needs during the Development Stage (1) up to Zero stage (2). Scrutinize every possible way to get what you need free, or for the least possible cost. Chapter 7 will discuss ways to minimizing cash outflow. Chapter 17 on raising money will dig deeper into quantifying your financial needs.
Zero Stage to Nonsuccess **(2) ➡ (3)** All fixed and variable cash outflows to grow your business, including inventory, infrastructure, labor, sales, marketing, administration, etc.	Estimate your financial needs from Zero stage (2) to Nonsuccess (3).
Breakeven Sales **(4)** YOU MADE IT!!!	Your company is cash flow positive from operations. Now, growth capital is required. Well done!

Source: www.CompetitiveSuccess.com, "Stages of Financial Needs and Potential Losses." Copyright © 2000 by Michael E. Gordon. Used with permission. *A blank version of this page can be downloaded from www.trumpuniversity.com /entrepreneurship101 for your personal use.*

future of your family or yourself at risk. However, if we are talking about sacrificing a new SUV ($35,000), a family vacation ($10,000), two cups of coffee a day ($1,750 annually), smoking ($1,500 annually), Milk Street Café chocolate chip cookies (now that would be a huge sacrifice for me), or . . . (add your own sacrifice here), it again comes down to the strength of your entrepreneurial driving force. Some ideas:

- Bootstrap to minimize costs (Chapter 7). Be a penny pincher.
- Strive to mobilize free resources, equipment, and people.

- Don't quit your day job. Develop your business evenings and weekends.
- Spend the minimum on development and start-up costs until you know you are on the right track.
- Get one or more partners.
- Other ideas that you can implement? Brainstorm.

Suggestion: If financial risk is your real concern, pause here, mark this page, and fill in Exhibit 3.1. Come up with some ballpark figures for potential financial loss through points (1) and (3). Approximations are better than nothing at all. Time spent quantifying your financial exposure would be time very well spent. Take it step by step.

Obstacle 3. Career Risks: Burning Bridges, Loss of Income Stream, Loss of Work Environment

This is an easy one. If you succeed in building your own profitable Money Machine, you will have created the most fantastic tailor-made career imaginable. You will also have selected your own community of coworkers. You can't ask for anything better. In my second business, I wanted to handle international marketing and still run the company as CEO. Building a strong organizational infrastructure was needed—one that could function without me for periods of time while I was traveling. What more could I have wanted—traveling the globe, running international trade shows, meeting with distributors and customers around the world. It would have been quite unlikely for me to have gotten that kind of heavenly job without being my own boss. The second point is this: Don't quit your day job until you have verifiable confirmation (Chapter 6) that your opportunity is real and that you have resources ready and available. This goes back to the previous point on financial risk management.

Obstacle 4. Emotional: Lack of Self-Confidence, Self-Perception If Your Business Is Not Successful

Self-confidence comes from succeeding, so go for it. If you don't jump into the Trying Game, you might go through life feeling the absence of self-confidence and self-esteem. And even if your first few attempts are non-successes (remember: no failures), your self-perception will *increase* because of what you are learning and the fact that you had the courage to keep trying, like Thomas Edison. And like Edison, you will succeed. Just go carefully, keep trying, and watch your cash flow.

Obstacle 5. Pressure on the Family, Not Enough Time

For me, it was really important to find the balance between my entrepreneurial pursuit and my strong family passion. When I was starting my first business, my children were young, and I deeply missed the time that could have been spent with them. I tried to involve the family in my activities where possible, and I looked for creative ways to spend family time, collectively and individually. My father had died during that time also, and my entire family needed emotional support. Awareness and sensitivity make it possible to find the balance.

Obstacle 6. Health, Stress, Long Hours

Whenever you are getting burned out, relax. Exercise, eat healthy, unwind with family and friends, get involved in activities, meditate, sing, play, listen to music, laugh, dance, go to movies, read . . . but don't lose sight of your entrepreneurial focus. *FIND THE BALANCE!*

Obstacle 7. Lack of the Big Opportunity

The topic of *opportunity* is a central theme in entrepreneurship, and it will be treated in depth in Chapters 5 and 6. In these chapters, you will learn how to search for ideas, and then to screen out the losers and identify the potential winning opportunity. By Chapter 19, you will have launched your business.

Obstacle 8. Minimal Tolerance for Risk in General

Ask yourself what specific risks are intolerable. Separate them into small pieces so that you can gain clarity. There are a few ways to look at risk tolerance. One is *Gordon's 1/5,000 Rule:* Years ago I figured out how to get comfortable with the risk-reward trade-offs in my own life. Example: One of my passions is traveling and experiencing the wonders of our world. So what is my risk tolerance for flying? What if one plane in one million goes down? One in 100,000? One in 1,000? One in 100? I concluded that my risk comfort zone for flying is about 1/5,000. Living with absolute fear, zero risk tolerance, would prevent me from pursuing my passion for travel. What kind of a life is that? Planes do go down on rare occasions, but does that mean I would never fly?

This thought process carries through to other kinds of risks as well. Venture capital firms invest in ventures that have homerun potential, and yet they know that only 20 percent of their portfolio companies are likely to have a significant payoff. They will succeed only once in five investments. But when they do, it's BIG. In baseball, the top batters hit one time in three, giving them a very attractive batting average of 0.33. In nature, the hawk succeeds only once in 10 attempts to capture its prey. Wouldn't that be true for you also? Start playing the Trying Game, but watch your cash flow like a hawk.

Obstacle 9. Inertia, "Just Plain Stuck"

This happens to everyone. What is causing your "justplainstuckness"? Brainstorm with friends. Ask them to help you define and overcome your inertia. Consider bringing in a business partner. Personally, when I get just plain stuck, my frustration goes sky high and *I have to do something*. And that's my advice to you. Do something! Take one extremely small, frugal step in *any* likely entrepreneurial direction. Action will lead you out of the wilderness.

Obstacle 10. I Still Don't Think I Have What It Takes to Be an Entrepreneur

As mentioned in the preceding chapter, everyone has the potential to learn and enhance their 11 Essential Entrepreneurial Power Skills. As your toolbox of traits fills up, you may gain the confidence to jump into the Trying Game. In any case, you will feel more in control of your life, more powerful and less powerless. Absorb the Essential Entrepreneurial Power Skills; set a course of action to master each skill.

Now for my promise: Study the book through Chapter 6. Don't continue reading beyond Chapter 6 until you have identified an authentic, honest-to-goodness, credible entrepreneurial opportunity. You have my personal guarantee that you will succeed. It is not possible to have a bona fide opportunity in hand and not launch it. Your entrepreneurial passion will drive you at harrowing speed to Chapter 19: "Launch Your Venture!".

These 10 obstacles are summarized in Exhibit 3.2. It would be time well spent to crawl through this chart. Fill out the severity and priority of each particular risk. Then figure out how to minimize or eliminate each concern. This is an excellent opportunity to use your brainstorming skills.

Downloadable Exhibit 3.2   Table of Obstacles and Risks*

	Concerns/Obstacles/Risks	Severity	How to Minimize
1.	Lack of financial resources: Minimal personal assets and borrowing ability.		
2.	Potential for financial loss: Start-up capital and cash outflow after zero stage.		
3.	Career risks: Loss of income stream, loss of job environment, burning bridges with employer.		
4.	Emotional: Lack of self-confidence; self-perception if business is not successful.		
5.	Pressure on family: Not enough time or financial resources.		
6.	Health: Stress, long hours.		
7.	Lack of the Big Opportunity.		
8.	Minimal tolerance for risk in general.		
9.	Inertia: "Just Plain Stuck."		
10.	"I still don't think I have what it takes to be an entrepreneur."		

Source: www.CompetitiveSuccess.com, "Table of Obstacles and Risks." Copyright © 2000 by Michael E. Gordon. Used with permission. *A blank version of this page can be downloaded from www.trumpuniversity.com/entrepreneurship101 for your personal use.*

Brainstorming as a Powerful
Problem-Solving Tool

On several occasions, I have alluded to brainstorming[1] as a technique to help you move beyond your obstacles. Brainstorming is a group thinking process that is used to generate creative ideas and to solve complex problems. Here's how it works: A group of imaginative, positive, and willing people come together to help you. A discussion leader, someone other than you, defines the problem, communicates the rules, and maintains the momentum. These are the rules to be followed by the group:

- Put a chart on the wall with a concise statement of the problem to be solved. Then encircle the problem with several other questions, as we did in Obstacle 1. These "what to, how to, when to" questions become calls to action.
- Get the ideas flowing. Absolutely no criticism or judgment of any kind (good or bad) of other ideas is permitted.
- Quantity of ideas is preferable to quality.
- Ideas are recorded and made visible during the session.
- Invent ideas to the "void," until there are no more ideas to come forth.
- Place no restrictions on ideas, be completely spontaneous. Nothing is too far-fetched when you're thinking way outside the box.
- Encourage one idea to build on another.
- Resist becoming committed to any one idea.
- Avoid defending any idea.
- Avoid repeating any idea, as if to give it credibility.

At the end of the brainstorming session, the nuggets are selected from the slag through refinement, combination, and improvement.

In one such session, a group came together to brainstorm the obstacle of lack of financial resources to help an anxious entreprenreuter-to-be. The issue was encircled with action-oriented questions: where to look for start-up and growth capital; how to proceed so that money is not show-stopping or limiting; what can be done to move forward with minimal financial resources? Exhibit 3.3 is the output of the brainstorming session.

Remember there are no "dumb" ideas in the brainstorming phase. Even seemingly ridiculous ideas are given respect, because they lead to energy, out-of-the-box thinking, humor, and unpredictable connections. Stealing, gambling, and begging get filtered out in the selection process.

Exhibit 3.3   Brainstorming the Lack of Financial Resources

Brainstorming by group of knowledgeable friends and advisors:

The obstacle: "Lack of financial resources is holding me back." (Encircling questions: *Where can I look for start-up and growth capital? How can I proceed so that money does not stop or limit me? What do I have to do to move forward with my limited financial resources?*)

Get loan from parents, get advice from SCORE (part of the Small Business Administration), get collateralized loan from bank, find business partners, use several personal credit cards, gamble, cash out your life insurance policy, borrow from friends, borrow from personal savings, get a second job, hold a contest or raffle, ask distant family members for money, sell off assets on eBay, buy lottery tickets, find a private angel investor, find venture capital, get a student loan, beg for donations, lease equipment, use other people's credit, hold an auction, go to foreclosure sales, go to pawnbrokers, obsess over cash flow, try barter and other noncash solutions, negotiate for everything, become a street musician at Harvard Square, collect stuff on trash pick-up day to resell, ask your landlord to invest, buy a business rather than starting one, bootstrap everything, sell to future customers at significant discount, apply for grants, figure out who you know who knows someone who knows someone, and so on.

Source: www.CompetitiveSuccess.com, "Brainstorming the Lack of Financial Resources." Copyright © 2000 by Michael E. Gordon. Used with permission.

The entrepreneur selected the following ideas to pursue:

- Get a temporary second job.
- Cash out his life insurance policy.
- Sell all unwanted personal assets on eBay.
- Borrow from family members.
- Look for a partner.

The important thing to note here is the power of the brainstorming process, not only for this exercise, but for every obstacle that must be overcome, every problem to be solved, and every complex decision to be made. The group intellect and experience is vastly greater than that of any one person.

Now that you see the power of brainstorming, use it abundantly.

SUMMARY

In this chapter, you have come to understand the 10 categories of obstacles that could be holding you back. Each obstacle has been examined and quantified where possible, with the goal of eliminating all roadblocks. You have learned the power of brainstorming to help solve complex problems and make the best decisions.

Actions

√ Study the Table of Obstacles and Risks (Exhibit 3.2) and rate the severity of your particular concerns.

√ Focus on those that are blocking you, and make a commitment to understand and eliminate them by using your brainstorming skills.

√ Don't permit yourself to be stopped. You are unstoppable!

Pep Talk

One of my favorite writers, Shakti Gawain, [2] *sums up my feelings:*

Your Life Is Your Work of Art

I like to think of myself as an artist, and my life is my greatest work of art. Every moment is a moment of creation, and each moment of creation contains infinite possibilities. I can do things the way I have always done them, or I can look at all the different alternatives, and try something new and different and potentially more rewarding. Every moment presents a new opportunity and a new decision.

What a wonderful game we are playing, and what a magnificent art form.

4

START RIGHT—BUILD ON
THE CUSTOMER MODEL

Why do some businesses succeed and others fail? I have asked myself that question throughout my 30-year career in entrepreneurship, consulting, and teaching. I arrived at the answer by asking the question in the form of the following equation:

$$\text{Competitive Success} = a + b + c + \ldots + n$$

This simple yet potent equation states that the keys to the success of your business will depend on a limited number of critical factors. Every great cook knows the importance of the recipe. If even one crucial ingredient is missing, the soufflé will be in jeopardy. Take away any one of the six strings from Andrés Segovia's Spanish guitar, and the concert stops. If even one of the necessary success factors is ignored, your business will suffer. On the other hand, if you really pay attention to these determinants, you will maximize the chances of achieving your one goal: creating and building a profitable, sustainable Money Machine.

So what are the keys to the success of your venture? Here are the essential factors that must capture your undivided attention as you grow your company:

Competitive Success = C + U + S + T + O + M + E + R

The CUSTOMER model is an acronym, and its meaning is summarized in Exhibit 4.1. There are a total of nine factors for competitive success when you include the most important factor: the customer himself or herself. These factors will be continuing themes throughout this book, and they will provide the scaffolding on which to build your company. Let's look at each of the nine factors.

GORDON's CUSTOMER MODEL: NINE FACTORS FOR COMPETITIVE SUCCESS

It is self-evident. There is no such thing as a business without willing buyers of your products and services. If you rivet your attention on customer satisfaction, success will likely follow. Likely, but without guarantees. What *can* be guaranteed is that your company cannot be built on customer dissatisfaction. There just aren't enough apathetic customers out there. Every customer you don't get, or that you lose, is a customer that one of your competitors gains. You can use the *customer-centricity*[1] of your

Downloadable Exhibit 4.1   Gordon's CUSTOMER Model: Nine Factors for Competitive Success*

C ulture	Shared beliefs, all-for-one, can-do, customer-centered
U niqueness	Innovative value creation in *every* aspect of your company
S trategy	Building sustainable, profitable competitive advantages
T echnology	Breakthroughs, disruptions, differentiation, productivity
O pportunity	Satisfying customer needs constantly and profitably
M anagement	*Leadership*, executive team, managers, supervisors
E xecution	Accomplishing the vision through strategic initiatives
R esources	People, financial, infrastructure, knowledge, physical, ...

Source: www.CompetitiveSuccess.com, "Gordon's CUSTOMER Model: Nine Factors for Competitive Success." Copyright © 2000 by Michael E. Gordon. Used with permission. ***This exhibit can be downloaded from www.trumpuniversity.com /entrepreneurship101 for your personal use.***

company as a competitive advantage. Chapter 18 will build on the development of a customer-centered culture. All other things being equal, the customer relationship itself is a competitive advantage.

Culture

Culture is the human side of your company. It is all about your team and how they interact, their shared beliefs, how they solve problems, their winning spirit, their priorities and attitudes toward customers, toward each other, and toward all stakeholders. Look at some of the great team cultures and you can readily see how this factor becomes a competitive advantage: Toyota, Southwest Airlines, the New England Patriots. Can you truly build a successful company by ignoring the culture of your company?

Uniqueness

Being unique is the heart and soul of entrepreneurship. The success of your company will depend on your ability to beat out your competition for share-of-market, and to become the preferred supplier of products and services. The customer makes choices: "To which competitor will I award this purchase order?" Your challenge is to stand out, to be different in ways that the customer values. And uniqueness must go beyond your products and services. Innovation and creativity must be harnessed to add unique value in _every_ aspect of your business.

Strategy

Strategy converts your opportunity into a profitable Money Machine. Strategy aims to achieve sustainable financial performance by differentiating your products, services and business methods from those of your competition—being different in a way that your customers value. Strategy includes everything you must do to capture and satisfy customers, into the future, while making healthy profits. There are many approaches to gaining strategic competitive advantages (see Chapter 12):

- Becoming the low-cost provider of products and services
- Developing differentiated, innovative products and services that have significant value to your customer
- Targeting a narrow niche: industry, geography, products, or services

- Employing a variety of differentiated business methods and approaches such as:
  —Offering unsurpassed customer service
  —Developing strong customer relationships
  —Nurturing an entrepreneurial company culture
  —Building unique core capabilities
  —Commercializing proprietary know-how
  —Erecting barriers to future competitor entry
  —Acting decisively to gain first-mover advantage
  —Gaining unique access to markets and channels of distribution
  —Running faster, trying harder
- Implanting all nine factors of Gordon's CUSTOMER model into your company

Can you truly build a successful company by ignoring strategic planning and implementation?

Technology

When you think of technology, the words that come to mind are likely to be *cutting-edge, breakthrough, disruptive, black box, nanoeverything*. Every year, MIT's *Technology Review* magazine features "Ten Technologies That Will Change the World." In 2003, these technologies were mechatronics, glycomics, quantum cryptography, and molecular imaging, to name a few. The following year, 10 new technologies were reported, and last year, 10 more. In spite of my science background, I have difficulty understanding most of them. *And yet they will change my future world!* And that is a small fraction of research that is going on in corporations and universities throughout the world. If you are actually building a high-technology company, this hyper-technological pace will keep your corporate paranoia churning. If you are building a nontechnology company, your challenge is to use the most effective state-of-the-art technology to improve infrastructure, productivity, and product and service delivery costs, to differentiate your company and disrupt your competition. Can you truly build a successful company by ignoring the technological tools that are constantly emerging?

Opportunity

The concept of opportunity is a central theme in entrepreneurship. Opportunities have the potential to create or add unique, differentiated value for the customer, and at the same time to generate significant profits for you. But opportunities are not easy to find. Every entrepreneur-to-be, every student of entrepreneurship, and most companies are searching. They are looking for sluggish competitors, rapidly growing markets, new technologies, and changes of any kind. And our hyperchanging world presents commercial possibilities like never before for the entrepreneurial opportunity seeker. Can you truly build a successful company by not proactively seeking and commercializing new opportunities? (See Chapter 6.)

Management

I am referring to all levels of management in your company: you as the *leader*, your executive team, managers, line supervisors, board of directors, and advisors. As CEO, you are responsible for creating a high-performance management structure throughout your organization. So what are *your* leadership functions?

- Establishing the vision and mission for your company
- Leading your company through the changes in today's rapidly developing world; responding to opporturnities and threats
- Developing an effective, motivated, high-performance corporate culture
- Training your management team and line supervisors
- Managing financial performance: sales growth, profits, return on equity, return on investment, sustainability
- Formulating and implementing an astute strategic plan
- Building and allocating resources
- Setting the moral tone of the company
- Managing risk
- Communicating continuously to all levels of your company

Can you truly build a successful company by ignoring management performance throughout the company, beginning with yourself as the leader?

Execution

Execution[2] is the process that makes your vision a reality. Once you have clarity on your strategic plan, your task is to ingrain strategic initiatives into your daily operations. To illustrate the use of strategic initiatives,

3M's strategic plan called for the creation of a passionate, innovative entrepreneurial culture. 3M accomplished this by allowing their researchers to use 15% of their time to work on *any* entrepreneurial idea they chose—no strings attached. This is a strategic initiative. Another example: 3M wanted to make sure their divisional CEOs were focusing on the commercialization of new products. To execute on this plan, 3M issued a strategic initiative linking the divisional CEOs' compensation to revenues generated from new products—specifically, 30% of annual sales had to come from new products commercialized within the previous 3 years. Other initiatives of 3M were based on financial metrics such as sales growth, profits, return on equity and return on investment. Can you truly build a successful company without the unwavering execution of your strategic plan?

Resources

Resources are anything, absolutely anything, that can move your venture further and faster, and with least risk. Resources fall into six categories: human, financial, physical, knowledge, infrastructure, and your imagination: a miscellaneous category containing any and all other resources that can make the difference between your success and nonsuccess. Imagination resources includes your Personal Power, access to international markets, your strong brand, ability to develop new products, key suppliers, unique core competencies, access to door openers, barriers to future entrants, your ability to negotiate, and your unstoppability. Even your ability to garner all necessary resources is a resource. Can you truly build a successful company without nurturing, mobilizing, and allocating powerful resources?

THE CUSTOMER MODEL IS HOLISTIC

It is important to note that each of the nine factors in the CUSTOMER model does not stand alone. All elements are intertwined for the performance of your company, as shown in Figure 4.1.

In specific situations, however, usually just a few of the factors come into play. By way of example, our static control company faced a problem that needed resolution. One of our strongest distributors was blocking us from direct contact with our own customers. The distributor was so dominant in this territory and was doing so much business for us (50% of

Figure 4.1 Gordon's Holistic CUSTOMER Model: Nine Factors for Competitive Success

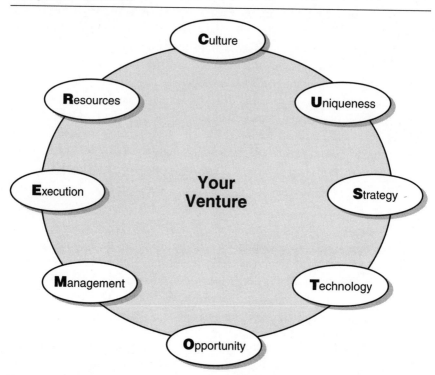

Source: www.CompetitiveSuccess.com, "Gordon's Holistic CUSTOMER Model." Copyright © 2000 by Michael E. Gordon. Used with permission.

our total company sales), that our hands seemed to be tied. However, we realized that we could never gain competitive success as a company without direct access to our own customers. How does the CUSTOMER model come into play? We reached a decision by focusing on Opportunity, Strategy, Management, and Culture. The Opportunity for us was to cement strong relationships with our customer base. Our Strategic decision was that we could not be prevented from dealing with our own customers in this, or in any territory. The Management team was brought into these discussions over many months to help shape the decision. The process of seeking input from our managers over a period of time nurtured a Culture based on respect for their opinions. And the result? We quickly hired three direct salespeople. We lost the distributor, and with him went 15% of our company sales, not 50%! Within one year, we had increased our business in this territory by 40%. The answers came from the CUSTOMER.

SUMMARY

This chapter develops Gordon's CUSTOMER Model, the nine factors for competitive success.[3] If you pay attention to all nine factors, you will maximize your company's chance of thriving into the far future:

C ulture	Shared beliefs, all-for-one, can-do, customer-centered
U niqueness	Innovative value creation in _every_ aspect of your company
S trategy	Building sustainable, profitable competitive advantages
T echnology	Breakthroughs, disruptions, differentiation, productivity
O pportunity	Satisfying customer needs constantly and profitably
M anagement	_Leadership_, executive team, managers, supervisors
E xecution	Accomplishing the vision through strategic initiatives
R esources	People, financial, infrastructure, knowledge, physical, …

Action

√ Go to www.trumpuniversity.com/entrepreneurship101 and download an 8½ × 11″ presentation of Gordon's CUSTOMER model. Make copies for every person in your company, and tape them on the walls. Can you imagine the power of this action? Everyone in your organization will share your vision for the customer-centric company and the nine factors for competitive success.

5

Scour the World
for Ideas

I am a magnet for budding entrepreneurs. They seek me out to describe what they see as fantastic ideas for new businesses. Some of them are truly exceptional. Others are interesting but farfetched; still others are downright bizarre. Their quick pitch is usually delivered with an outpouring of passion, excitement, and hoopla. "I think this could be a truly great business!" they say.

If only they could read my mind. Still better that they would read this chapter and the next. We are going to discuss three of the book's most important concepts:

1. Finding business ideas (the process of *ideation*).
2. Examining the *fit* between the idea and your personal skills, passions, risk tolerance, and objectives.
3. Determining which of those ideas are true opportunities to start and grow a profitable, sustainable Money Machine.

Most entrepreneurs assume that their creative idea can be commercialized readily into a profitable business. Not so! Ideas are the starting

Donald Trump on Ideas and Opportunities

Ideas and opportunities are everywhere. I see them constantly. I have also built an organization to proactively search for and identify opportunities that are consistent with our overall strategy, and with the Trump brand for the ultimate in quality, luxury, sophistication and elegance. Donald Trump The Fragrance came in through my licensing group. This product is an excellent example of opportunity recognition, and how we are leveraging and monetizing the Trump brand. I am passionate about creating unequaled excellence. It is this process of finding ideas and identifying and commercializing opportunities that makes me so excited about entrepreneurship.

Photo courtesy of the Trump Organization.

point, but every idea must go through a rigorous distillation and selection process. The diamonds must be separated from the coal. Ideas and opportunities are not the same, and you need to understand the difference. If your idea is not an opportunity, not one minute, not one dollar should be spent on it—it's a nonstarter. But if you are sure that you have an opportunity, then step on the gas and use the rest of this book as your guide to success. If you are uncertain, there are ways to proceed cautiously, with small, frugal learning steps (Chapter 7).

FINDING BUSINESS IDEAS

Consider this example. My wife, Maria, was interested in being in her own business, so one bright spring day, we walked around town exploring businesses that appealed to her. I challenged her to look at every business on our itinerary and to ask herself three questions:

1. Is this a good business?
2. Is this a business that will capture my passions?
3. Can I add unique customer value to the business?

Maria took up the challenge with gusto, and many more questions danced in her mind.

We walked past at least 50 businesses that morning: a pizza shop, beauty salon, clothing store, jewelry store, a copy center, antiques consignment store, newspaper and magazine store, taqueria, flower shop, office supplies store, optician, sushi restaurant, coffee shop, used books store, hardware store, more restaurants, liquor store, candy store, and many, many others.

None interested her, and few seemed to have much potential for future growth. Suddenly, one business jumped out at Maria. She spied an interesting shop that sold an incredible variety of beads and patterns to do-it-yourself jewelry makers for necklaces, earrings, handbags, hats, gloves, and so on. We went inside and observed. We made mental notes on the number of customers, age, gender, time of day, and what they were buying. Then we bought some items and stood near the cash register to determine the size of each sale and to estimate the average customer purchase amount. We counted the number of sales over a 30-minute period.

Later, over coffee in a nearby bistro, we projected the hourly, daily, weekly, and annual sales of the bead shop. We guesstimated that sales for that location were in excess of $500,000, and that profit margins before expenses were in the neighborhood of 50 percent, meaning that for $100 of bead sales, the cost of the goods to the business is $50. (These financial concepts will be developed fully in Chapter 13.)

The business was attractive from several perspectives: repeat customers, nonperishable inventory, excellent location, potential for growth through additional locations, and it was a simple business to understand. Maria also felt that the business would engage her own artistic talents, and she liked the community of artistic people that were attracted to the store. Then, the most exciting thing of all happened: She said, "If I owned that shop, I would create a tight community of beading enthusiasts. They could hang out in my shop and share their beading interests in a comfortable social environment with coffee, tea, and snacks. I might call it The Beading Café, and have guest speakers, craft shows, a consignment store.

It would be the best beading shop in the area." Maria's creative juices were really flowing. She was thinking about how to *add unique value* for her customers.

Not bad for a two-hour walk!

This simple exercise presents an entrepreneurial model for idea searching and screening. Imagine a funnel. Maria was filling the top of the funnel with 50 or more business ideas, using her own judgments to screen out the unattractive ones, the uncomfortable ones, the one's that didn't *fit* her. Only one popped out the bottom. This chapter is about filling the top of your funnel with business ideas and looking for the *fit* between you and your personal objectives, skills, risk tolerance, and passions. The next chapter explains how to determine which of these ideas has real money-making potential.

Ideas Can Come from Anywhere

Fortunately, these are fertile times for self-starting, imaginative entrepreneurs. Our rapidly moving world presents us with a gold mine of ideas. If our world were not changing, we'd be living in a stagnant environment of mature markets, intense competition, and low profit margins. The entrepreneur in us says "Bring on the changes!" The challenge for you is to become *aware* and to constantly search your dynamic environment for new, different, better, and innovative ideas. Let your eyes roll around Figure 5.1 and imagine the wealth of possibilities that face you as our world undergoes these dramatic, disruptive, and turbulent changes.

An idea for a new venture can come from absolutely anywhere and everywhere. My own approach to idea generation is proactive, energetic, and purposeful. When the weather is accommodating, I ride my bike around my extended neighborhood, keeping my eyes open for real estate development opportunities. At the very least, I have a pleasant experience; at the very best, I spot an idea that may turn into a good business opportunity. Recently, for example, I identified two properties worth exploring. I also have three realtors looking for real estate deals for me. I crawl around www.brokerservicesnetwork.com frequently to search for businesses for sale. I attend stock investment meetings regularly to learn about high-potential, small public companies that are below the radar screen. The concept of the idea funnel is burned into my subconscious. I know

Figure 5.1 Turbulent Global Changes

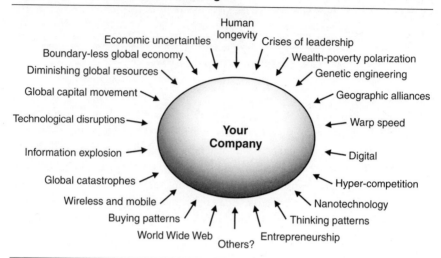

Source: www.CompetitiveSuccess.com, "Turbulent Global Changes." Copyright © 1998 by Michael E. Gordon. Used with permission.

that 50 to 100 ideas need to go into the top for a few good ones to pop out the bottom.

Let your eyes also roll around Figure 5.2. This diagram gives you places that abound with possibilities for ideas. You have your own idea-hunting grounds. Here are my 10 personal favorites:

1. Wherever my passions lead me.
2. Any trade show in an attractive industry.
3. Real estate and business opportunities in the *Banker and Tradesman* newspaper, *Investor's Business Daily* and *Wall Street Journal.*
4. Franchising shows.
5. Recognizing and borrowing other companies' best practices.
6. Magazines and catalogues such as *Inc., Entrepreneur, MIT Technology Review, Popular Electronics,* Edmund Scientific catalogue, and the like.
7. Unstoppable world trends; for example, energy shortages, the commercializing of Asia, population/demographics, the increasing U.S. national debt, global warming, the liftoff of digital, wireless, mobile, personal devices.
8. Brainstorming with my entrepreneurial friends.

Figure 5.2   Ideas Can Come from Anywhere

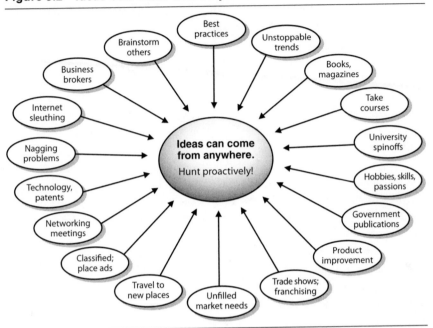

Source: www.CompetitiveSuccess.com, "Ideas Can Come from Anywhere." Copyright ©
1998 by Michael E. Gordon. Used with permission.

9. Figuring out what the world needs now as it goes through these
   dramatic changes.
10. Traveling the world and just observing.

Sometimes ideas just come your way; you need only to recognize their
potential and be willing to try them out. Consider this example: Edith
Beristain was eager to make a little extra money for her family. She and her
husband had three young children, and any supplementary income would
really help. Her nephew, Jesus, had found a source of high-quality, stylish
women's lingerie that could be bought directly from a manufacturer in
Mexico. The manufacturing company had an attractive catalogue for their
product line, with prices. Edith began showing the catalogue and some
lingerie to neighbors and friends. She made a few sales. She gave some catalogues to her husband to give to the secretaries where he worked. More
sales came in. Her daughters passed out catalogues to their friends at
school. Still more sales came in. She and her family were excited, and they

envisioned a point in the future where they might even have a store selling lingerie, handbags, cosmetics, and accessories; and a multilevel marketing program; and a lingerie web store; and . . .

Don't be limited to your own ideas. Some of the most successful individuals and companies got to the top by recognizing the significance of other people's ideas and borrowing shamelessly. Consider best practices, one of the most powerful entrepreneurial thoughts ever developed. Jack Welch, former CEO of General Electric, challenged and incentivized his people to find and apply the best business practices used in industry, no matter where in the world they were found. Welch recognized that you do not need to create your own ideas. You can absorb the best thinking, technology, processes, strategies, revenue models, product concepts, attitudes, and business cultures in the world. In essence, 6.3 billion people on our planet and millions of companies are doing the development for you. All you have to do is find and apply their best practices.

By way of example, consider Andy Wilson. He had reached the decision point in his life and career where he needed a significant change. Taking some time off to travel the country, he boarded a bus in search of himself and potential business ideas. In Memphis, Andy spied a strange-looking military vehicle that had been converted into a sightseeing tour bus. The machine was a World War II amphibious boat/truck known as a Duck. An imaginative Memphis entrepreneur had already built a tour business around these weird transports. Andy was captivated and began to explore the possibility of bringing this concept to Boston. The rest of the story is history! Today, Boston Duck Tours[1] is an immense commercial success. What is fascinating about this case is that it was not even Andy Wilson's idea. He saw its success somewhere else and recreated it in another location.

I am certainly not proposing that you copy or misuse any proprietary or intellectual property of other people or companies. If the information is readily available to the public, if you did not obtain it in devious ways, if it is not legally protected, you are free to absorb best practices. It is a two-way street; anyone can find and adopt your best practices—thus the need for urgency. Time is not your friend in our urgently competitive world.

EXAMINE THE FIT BETWEEN YOU AND YOUR IDEA

Now that you understand the process of searching for ideas, the next step is to explore *fit*. Does the idea fit with your personal skills, passions, risk tolerance, and objectives? Look inside yourself. There is already a template to test your comfort level when you think about your own business. As you consider the questions that follow, fill in Exhibit 5.1:

- What type of business would *fit* comfortably with you? When you envision yourself as CEO of your own company, what do you do, think and feel every day?
- What are your passions, interests, hobbies, spare-time activities? If you do not have boundless enthusiasm for your venture, your business won't make it.
- How does your idea fit with your risk tolerance? If your idea requires large amounts of capital, is it too risky for you? (Refer back to Chapter 3.)
- What kind of business activities do you enjoy most and least: marketing, sales, creating something with your own hands, manufacturing, operations, product development, finance, bookkeeping, international sales, product development, building your team, nurturing customer relationships, business development and strategy, leadership and general management, others? You certainly don't want your opportunity to lead you into the wrong career.
- What skills, resources, and experiences do you have or could gather that could be commercialized?
- What kind of business hooks you: products or services? You could sell tangible items such as sporting goods, clothing, books, jewelry, furniture, electronics, or you could perform services such as computer training, running networking meetings, consulting, or circuit board assembly.
- What about a virtual business over the Web, again providing either products or services? That is intriguing because your marketplace would be the limitless world.
- Do you have the knowledge for a technology business, or should you go the nontechnology route?
- Do you relate to a consumer business, interacting directly with the end user, or perhaps you could be a supplier of goods and services to other businesses?
- What about a socially conscious business, giving you the opportunity to do good for the world and do well financially at the same time?
- Would this be a full-time or part-time activity? You could start slowly, evenings and weekends, and let the business find its own trajectory.

Downloadable Exhibit 5.1   Table of Fit between You and Your Idea*

What Kinds of Ideas Fit You?	Your Comfort Zone
When you envision yourself as CEO, what does your company look and feel like?	
Does your idea *fit* with your passions, interests, hobbies, and spare-time activities?	
How does your idea fit with your tolerance for risk?	
What kinds of business activities do you enjoy most? Least?	
What skills and experiences do you have that could be commercialized?	
Do you prefer a product or a service business?	
What about tapping into world markets with a Web-based business?	
Do you have the skills for a technology business?	
Are you more interested in selling directly to consumers or to businesses?	
Are you passionate about a socially conscious or not-for-profit business?	
Do you want a full-time or part-time business?	
Do you foresee a smaller lifestyle business or a high-potential company?	
Are you interested in having partners, or do you prefer to go it alone?	
Is there a specific market that you can penetrate readily?	
Most important, how can you add value and fill the needs of your customers?	
Are there other specific fit questions for you to consider?	

Source: www.CompetitiveSuccess.com, "Table of Fit between You and Your Idea." Copyright © 2000 by Michael E. Gordon. Used with permission. ***A blank version of this page can be downloaded from www.trumpuniversity.com/entrepreneurship101 for your personal use.***

- Do you envision growing a smaller lifestyle business, or a high-potential company?
- Are you interested in having partners or going it alone?
- Is there a specific market that you can penetrate readily?
- Ultimately, shouldn't you focus primarily on your potential customers first and yourself second? How can you add unique value for your customers, satisfy their needs, and differentiate your products or services from your competitors'?
- Are there other, more creative questions that might lead you to the best fit between you and your idea? This is an ideal topic for a brainstorming session with your friends.

Three Entrepreneurs in Search of *Fit*

Stephen

Stephen was anxious to be in his own company, one close to where he lived. He became excited when he realized there were no fish supply stores in the area, and he began to pursue this idea. He borrowed money from family and friends and tapped his own personal finances and credit cards, for a total of $18,000. He found a location, signed a lease, stocked the store with tanks, supplies, accessories, and exotic fish of all kinds, and he opened the doors for business. Stephen was feeling really exhilarated. One year later, his business had to close due to lack of customers. Breakeven sales were not even in sight (Chapter 13). By the time he had extricated himself, losses amounted to almost $18,000.

What went wrong? For starters, Stephen knew nothing about the fish business. He never even owned a fish tank; it was not a hobby or a passion of his. Exotic fish are difficult to care for, and many died because of his lack of knowledge. There may or may not have been a local need. He didn't really know. In any case, customers were quite dissatisfied when they could not get thorough answers to their questions. What would you have done differently?

Adam

Adam loved to work with his hands. As a young boy, he tinkered with model airplanes, built his own workshop in the basement, and repaired furniture. He particularly liked to help his father with repair projects around the home. As he grew up, he did odd jobs for neighbors that involved building things. When he finished school, he took a job in a local contracting firm as a carpenter's assistant. Once he had two years of experience under his belt, Adam became the lead carpenter on several projects.

Before long, Adam came to believe that he could do contracting by himself—to be in his own building business. But he did not want to take the risk by quitting his day job. So he began taking on small weekend construction projects: a deck for his friend, a tree house for the neighbor's children, a spare room in the basement of a buddhist sangha. Six months later, Adam was so busy with weekend work that he decided to go for it. He is now running his own growing business. What did he do right? He followed his passion for building things and working with his hands; he gained skills and real-world experience through weekend projects as well as an apprenticeship; he minimized risk by keeping his day job.

Deborah

Deborah had a keen interest in being in her own business, but did not have a good idea. During her research on the Internet and at the local library, the concept of franchising got her attention. She began to read books and magazines about franchising, and the more she read, the more interested she became. Deborah then went to the National Franchise and Business Opportunities Show in Atlanta and was astounded to see all the potential opportunities available. She was particularly attracted to a senior care service business because of her compassionate, warm-hearted nature. Deborah had considerable experience ministering to her own aging parents. Also, she could run the business from her home and start quickly.

The franchising company had a proven track record and a brand name. It would give her training and guidance in starting and running her business. It was a turn-key operation. Also, she could afford the moderate franchising fee. And, the 5 percent royalty on sales didn't seem unreasonable. After diligently seeking advice from the Small Business Administration (www.sba.org) and talking to other successful franchise owners from this company, she bought a franchise. Without an idea of her own, she did it! Today Deborah's business is profitable and growing. She particularly enjoys the freedom of managing her own time and being her own boss.

The one lesson that you can take from Stephen, Adam, and Deborah is that the process of idea searching must be **P**roactive, **E**nergetic, and **P**urposeful. So many exceptional things have happened to me in my life because of my PEP. Success comes to those who are doing, not just thinking and talking. Often I look to nature to understand how various species survive and thrive. The more I observe, the greater is my sense of wonder at life. What comes to mind is the Trap Door spider. This amazing creature is as un-entrepreneurial as can be. He makes a nest just below the surface and overlays it with a very light top cover, with him inside. His "fingers" are positioned at the corners of the trap door, and when he feels vibration from an unsuspecting wandering bit of food, he flips the door open and pounces on his prey. There are two compelling reasons why you should never be a Trap Door spider:

1. Good things rarely come to entrepreneurs who wait patiently.
2. If your strongly held goal in life is to start and grow your own successful business, it just won't happen unless you are proactive to the extreme.

SUMMARY

This chapter is about proactively searching for business ideas, then screening them for personal fit. Fit takes into account your skills, passions, risk tolerance, and objectives. Does your idea *fit* you comfortably, and does it lead to your personal and business goals? Most important, how can you add unique value for the customer and differentiate your products and services from your competition?

Actions

√ Check your comfort zone in Exhibit 5.1. Get to know yourself.
√ Make a list of all of your favorite places to search for ideas.
√ Commit to stuffing 10 ideas per week into the top of the idea funnel. That's what I said: 10.
√ Go out there and do it!

Opportunity Recognition: The Trump Signature Collection

Photo courtesy of the Trump Organization.

Donald Trump and the Trump Organization are masters of opportunity recognition. By way of example, consider the Trump Signature Collection of suits, neckwear, dress shirts, cuff links, eyewear, sportswear, and timepieces. How did this business unit emerge? Ideas originate both internally and externally. Internally, the business strategy group plans new directions and business thrusts to be commercialized. Externally, ideas pour in from entrepreneurial companies seeking to participate in the leverage of the Trump brand for their products and services. Once a decision is made that a product is consistent with the overarching strategy, the Trump Organization's licensing group initiates the negotiation process. Years of experience have resulted in a deep knowledge of branding and marketing DNA. They negotiate sophisticated licensing contracts to bring the best deals to the table, seeking:

- Unsurpassed quality consistent with the Trump brand
- Synergy between the Trump strategy and the specific products and services
- Relationships with the best business partners
- Powerful channels of distribution
- Sustainable financial performance to name but a few of the key deal points*

* Discussions with Cathy Glosser, Licensing Department, in the Trump Organization, 2006.

6

SELECT ONE
(AND ONLY ONE)
OPPORTUNITY

You learned from the previous chapter that there is a difference between just any idea, and one that fits your personal objectives, skills,
risk tolerance, and passions. Now your task is to scrutinize the idea even
more closely to determine whether it is an entrepreneurial opportunity.
The term *opportunity* has a distinct meaning in entrepreneurship. Opportunities have inherent characteristics that enable them to be converted
into positive, sustainable Money Machines in the right hands and under
the right conditions. Consider the following case study of a real situation,
then ask yourself whether the two entrepreneurs, Mark and Larry, have a
true entrepreneurial opportunity.

CASE STUDY: PLASTECHNOLOGY[1]

MARCH 31, 2002

Even the most casual observer could see the stress and frustration carved on
their faces. Mark and Larry were sitting in Café Vittorio doing some deep
soul searching. They desperately wanted to be in business for themselves,

but couldn't figure out what to do and how to do it. "So, what should we do," asked Larry? "Should we take a chance and buy the equipment at auction tomorrow? Quit our jobs and go for it?" "But how could we support our families?" Mark asked. "Maybe we should just stop thinking about starting a business and give up our life dreams of being in business for ourselves. We could make a proposal to Printronics to let us create a precision molding division internally, but how would we be rewarded? I wish we could figure out a course of action. The risks seem overwhelming. I can't sleep."

THE IDEA

Mark Greene and Larry Quinn had worked at Printronics International Corporation in the Plastic Materials Development Department since 1999. Those were intense times for Printronics because their breakthrough color printing technology had been unveiled at the stockholders' meeting, but the announcement was premature. The product was not ready for commercialization. Many significant problems prevented Printronics from actually launching its new printer and cartridge system. Dr. Edward Lane, the CEO and inventor of the new technology, was driving the company very hard to solve the problems and to get the product to market. Mark and Larry were responsible for solving the quality control problems for all of the plastic components: precise gears, lenses, mirrors, cams, the housing, the print head, and more. They traveled around the country, working with plastics manufacturers to develop process specifications, select materials, design the molds, perform component testing, and refine quality control procedures.

After three years of this intensive traveling, Mark and Larry wondered why there were so many persistent manufacturing problems. Mark pondered, "If we could not find competent molders for Printronics, perhaps the industry needs a sophisticated manufacturer of small, custom injection-molded plastic parts for very demanding applications. I am sure there are many, many customers that have needs similar to Printronics'." They had confidence in their knowledge and concluded that this was a good idea for a business. The possibilities of launching their own business and filling this unmet market need seemed limitless. They had even thought of a name for their company: Plastechnology, Inc.

MARK GREENE

Mark, 34 years old, graduated from the University of Florida with a bachelor's degree in biology. He spent two years at DuPont Plastics Company working on improved bio-compatible materials as a development chemist.

Currently, he is the manager of the Plastic Materials Development Department at Printronics International Corporation. Mark has a wife and two children—Adam, 5, and Debbie, 2 years old. They live in their own modest home, which has a sizable mortgage. Recently, Mark's father became seriously ill and his mother required considerable emotional support. Mark's family life is very important to him.

LARRY QUINN

Larry, 31 years old, graduated from Lowell Polytechnic Institute with a degree in Plastic Engineering. He is a development engineer in the Plastic Materials Development Department at Printronics. Throughout his professional career, Larry has distinguished himself as a creative product and process development engineer. Larry's family life revolves around his mortgaged home in the suburbs, his wife Katrina, his dog Winston, and his children—Ingrid, 3, and Amber, 1 year old. Mark and Larry have grown to be very close friends as well as productive colleagues.

INJECTION MOLDING

Injection molding is a high-volume manufacturing process that is capable of producing a wide variety of plastic parts from a broad range of plastic materials. In operation, plastic pellets are placed in the hopper of the injection-molding machine and conveyed along the barrel under conditions of high temperature and pressure. The molten plastic is then injected into a single- or multicavity mold, which is the negative image of the desired part. The molten plastic is allowed to solidify in the mold until the part is stable and can then be ejected. One machine has the capability of producing millions of parts per year.

Applications for plastic injection molding are limitless. Virtually every sector of the economy uses plastic injection-molded parts: medical, automotive, sports, recreation, electronics, custom industrial components, toys, and other consumer products. Because plastics are so ubiquitous, the industry is well developed and very mature. In fact, there is intense rivalry between injection-molding companies. Price undercutting is one main way for companies to try to gain competitive advantage. The customer owns the molds, and he can remove them at any time and place the work with another molder.

There are thousands of custom injection molders in the United States, and most of them struggle to be profitable. They range from unsophisticated garage shops to highly sophisticated, highly instrumented manufacturing operations. The industry segment that Mark and Larry have identified is the demanding end of the market for small, custom injection-molded plastic parts requiring close tolerance, lot-to-lot precision, and unique materials. The market characteristics can be described as regional, engineering-oriented, equipment-intensive, and strongly competitive. And in today's global economy, the outsourcing of custom molded plastics by the customer to Asia, Mexico, and Eastern Europe is becoming easier.

THE AUCTION

Used molding equipment can be purchased from dealers, from private molders with excess equipment, and through auctions. Although it is cheaper to purchase at auction, there are no warranties. The equipment is sold as is. The molding equipment that Mark and Larry had seen at the auction preview was older technology, larger machines than they had in mind, dismantled, but they were quite affordable. They estimated that they could buy the equipment for $6,500. If they bought the same equipment brand new, the price would be more than $200,000. Pooling their personal and family resources, they could come up with $15,000, but if they didn't purchase the equipment at auction, they had no idea how they could finance anything more expensive.

MARCH 31, 2002

"Okay, Larry. It's decision time. Tomorrow, April Fool's Day, is the auction. What are we going to do?" Mark had a lump in his throat from the excitement and uncertainty as he envisioned his future.

Question: Do Mark and Larry have an entrepreneurial opportunity, and if so, how should they pursue it?

This case raises several other questions as well:

- What risks confront Mark and Larry?
- Are they truly entrepreneurs? Are they capable of actually starting this business?
- Should they make a proposal to Printronics to start this venture internally? If so, what is the proposal, and what about their roles and rewards?

- Should they buy the equipment at auction?
- How should they raise additional money for this venture?
- Would you invest if they approached you for capital?
- What are their next steps?

This is a true story. I know Mark and Larry very well and have consulted with them on these agonizing decisions. They are typical of many passionate, motivated, frustrated potential entrepreneurs. Maybe the exact situation does not match yours, but aren't you facing the same issues? Obstacles, risks, financial obligations, self-doubt, resource limitations, family responsibilities, indecision, lack of understanding about the differences between ideas and opportunities?

Suggestion: Pause here, mark this page, and consider the case questions and your answers. Reframe them so that they apply to your specific situation. What would you do in a similar set of circumstances? Focus on whether this is an opportunity for Mark and Larry. If not, they must restructure their original idea, or go back to the previous chapter on ideation.

At the moment of the case, there are four possible scenarios that might befall them, or you in similar circumstances (refer to Figure 6.1):

Figure 6.1   Four Possible Scenarios

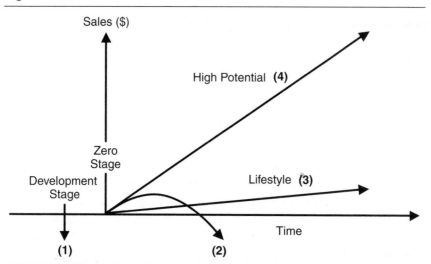

Source: www.CompetitiveSuccess.com, "Four Possible Scenarios." Copyright © 2002 by Michael E. Gordon. Used with permission.

1. *Scenario (1):* They could decide not to purchase the equipment and abandon the Plastechnology idea. Admittedly the decision could be delayed into the future, but for now, let's assume that in Scenario (1), Plastechnology is a nonstarter, and does not emerge from the development stage.
2. *Scenario (2):* Mark and Larry purchase the equipment and build a plastics injection-molding factory and get limited sales. But limited sales force the company to close.
3. *Scenario (3):* Plastechnology becomes a reality and grows to the level of a lifestyle business, providing Mark and Larry with a fulfilling quality of life in their own business, as well as the satisfaction of being their own bosses. Sales grow to $500,000 to $1 million. Very exciting!
4. *Scenario (4):* Plastechnology has found a sweet spot in the injection-molding market. Revenues skyrocket to $10 million within a 5- to 10-year period, making it a high-potential company.

In your judgment, which scenario actually happened?

Like a soap opera, the story of Plastechnology will unfold throughout this book. Stay tuned, but don't rush ahead until you have answered the case questions.

WHAT *IS* THE DIFFERENCE BETWEEN AN IDEA AND AN OPPORTUNITY?

There is a shorter answer and a longer answer to this question. The shorter answer is this: Any idea that can actually become a positive, sustainable Money Machine is an opportunity. If that seems like circular reasoning, it is. But all the well-crafted logic and analysis cannot dispute a successful outcome. Success tells the whole story. Let me share two stories from thousands of everyday examples that make this point.

Ed Marram[2] started his one-person consulting company in 1979 out of need. He had no job and little money, but he did have some experience working as a government contractor. Ed describes his situation: "I was motivated by necessity. I would go to Washington to find out what projects the different government agencies were funding. I would then write up proposals for the ones I thought I could satisfy." If he won the contract, he would set up some laboratory equipment and perform experiments. Over a 25-year period, his company, Geo-Centers, Inc., grew rapidly because of his hard work, good decisions, and dogged persistence. On several occasions, his company was listed as one of America's fastest growing companies by Inc. magazine. By the time Ed sold Geo-Centers in 2005, there were 1,200 employees, four divisions, and 17 locations.

Mellanie Stephens[3] had no job, but she did have two skills. She could sew and she could sell. From that humble beginning, she began making canvas bags for sailors, then cotton pants, and then an entire line of comfortable lifestyle clothing. By the seventh year, she had built the Kettle Creek Canvas Company, which had over 40 franchisees and $10 million in sales and had become a dominant branded player in the Canadian clothing market.

Many, many more stories could be told—LL Bean, Esprit, Nantucket Nectars, Burt's Bees—where the startups were so small, so nondramatic, and so unlikely to have led to huge successes.

At what point did these situations represent real business opportunities? They certainly did not appear to be anything unusual at the outset. Did Ed's phenomenal growth and Mellanie's commercialization of her sewing and selling skills share some things in common? Definitely! Need, desire, passion—plus the ability of the founders to work hard and smart, to take calculated risks, to evolve, to adapt, to make good decisions, and to never give up. These personal power skills will be continuing themes in this book: Anyone who refuses to be stopped will succeed. Therefore, if success is defined as actually creating a cash-positive business, *almost any* (but not every) idea is a potential opportunity in the right hands because the founding entrepreneurs will continuously refine, shape, reposition, modify, and retool it. They will never give up on their dream to create their own business, even though their first attempts are nonsuccesses. They will eventually succeed by their willpower and skillpower.

Now comes the longer answer. What characterizes an entrepreneurial opportunity? How can you know in advance whether your idea is just another rough thought or if it truly presents an opportunity to build a successful business? You cannot know definitively, but you can certainly shift the odds in your favor. Look at the Opportunity Screening Funnel (Figure 6.2) as a means of visualizing this extraction process. Pay particular attention to the nine screening categories.

Figure 6.2   Opportunity Screening Funnel

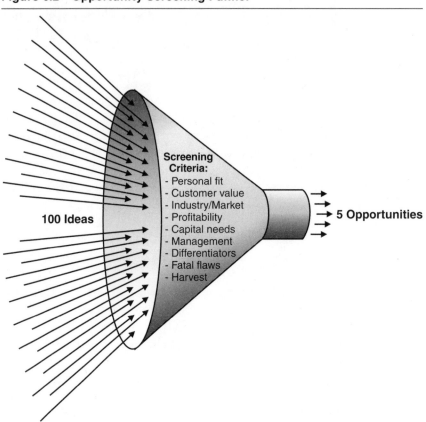

Source: www.CompetitiveSuccess.com, "Opportunity Screening Funnel." Copyright ©
2005 by Michael E. Gordon.

   In the previous chapter, your idea was examined for personal *fit* between your objectives, skills, risk tolerance, and passions. That was the
easy test. Your opportunity must now overcome eight more demanding
hurdles, like a salmon swimming upstream in a swift, steep river to reach
its spawning ground. The Opportunity Screening Checklist in Exhibit 6.1
provides an outline of these multidimensional factors that have been
shown to characterize entrepreneurial opportunities.[4] As you go through
the list, check or double check the ones that apply to your idea, X or XX
the ones that don't, and put question marks next to the uncertain ones.
Your goal is to come away from this exercise with a go/no-go decision on
whether to commit resources in pursuit of your opportunity.

Downloadable Exhibit 6.1   Opportunity Screening Checklist*

Category	Checklist Questions	Rating/Comments × ? √
Personal fit	- Is there a *fit* between your idea and your personal skills, passions, risk tolerance, and objectives? (Refer to Chapter 5 on Ideas.)	
Customer and product issues	- Does your product or service eliminate a nagging problem for your customer? - Is it innovative, creative, differentiated? - Does it add significant, unique, cost-effective value for your customer?	
Market dynamics	- Is the market large and growing? - Is the industry favorable in terms of competitors, buyers, suppliers, substitutes, and future entrants? - Can you gain market share because of untapped market niches, weak and fragmented competitors, and reachable customers?	
Profitability and scalability	- Is there a strong and profitable customer need, want, and demand? - Is there the potential for recurring profitable sales? - How sensitive is the market to product pricing? - Can you reach breakeven sales and positive cash flow rapidly? - Does your business have the ability to expand rapidly with manageable risk?	
Capital issues	- Do you require large amounts of capital to start and grow your business? - Is your business capable of showing an attractive return on investment for yourself and for other investors?	
Management team	- Do you and your team have industry knowledge, skills and experience, integrity, strong entrepreneurial traits (Chapter 2), and **unstoppability**?	

(continued)

Exhibit 6.1   Continued

Category	Checklist Questions	Rating/Comments × ? ✓
Competitive advantages and differentiators	- Does your business have many points of competitive strength: strong customer relationships, breakthrough technology, a strong brand, or the right timing? - Will your business be the low-cost producer, the most differentiated producer, or both? - Do you have patents, or other barriers to entry? - Does your company have access to financial resources? - Does your company have access to channels of distribution? - Do you have an opportunity based on emerging trends, such as global market expansion, energy shortages, disruptive technology, new business methodology, the disruption of your competitors through the application of information technology, channels of outsourcing, or others?	
Fatal flaws (defects that cannot be changed)	- Are there particular defects in your business that cannot be surmounted: overpowering competition, cost of market entry, small size of market, lack of customer need/want, inability to deliver products and services at acceptable prices, or others?	
Harvest issues	- Will your business command a premium price when you are ready to sell, merge, or go public?	

Source: www.CompetitiveSuccess.com, "Opportunity Screening Checklist." Copyright © 2000 by Michael E. Gordon. Used with permission. ***A blank version of this page can be downloaded from www.trumpuniversity.com/entrepreneurship101 for your personal use.***

Having completed the checklist, you now understand why many entrepreneurs get stuck at the opportunity recognition stage. There are ??s and XXs all over the place. A perfect picture does not emerge. The good news is that you have screened out the obvious losers. Defective ideas give clear no-go signals. You also have gained experience in screening opportunities.

For those ideas that are attractive but still uncertain, you have a short list of items to research before making a decision.

What if you are still reluctant to commit financial resources to your idea-opportunity, even after doing more homework? You are just not sure. Now what? Let's go back to the fundamental question: *How can you know in advance whether your idea is just another rough thought or if it truly presents an opportunity to build a successful business?* The answer lies in your personal definition of "successful business," and this reduces down further to four *hows:* How big? How fast? How much risk? and How about your future? Read on, answer the four questions, and I will then tie them together with opportunity screening.

How Big?

Successful businesses come in a wide range of sizes, but the only thing that matters is what size feels successful to you: annual profitable sales of $100K; $500K; $1M; $5M; $10M; $50M? (Circle your choice: K = thousands, M = millions).

How Fast?

A very well-known company lost money for 14 years, having started on the wrong track. Five investors pooled some money and bought a corundum mine, hoping to produce abrasive grinding wheels. As their luck would have it, the quality of the corundum was too poor. They tried to make a go of it for years, and finally they changed direction to pulverize the stone and glue it to paper. The resulting product, sandpaper, gained sales slowly. Their next product was masking tape for the emerging automotive industry. Fourteen unprofitable years from launch, 3M (Minnesota Mining and Manufacturing Company) turned a profit, continued to grow slowly and steadily, and today, 104 years later, the company has sales in excess of $22 billion, a global geographic reach, 45 divisions, and more than 100 commercial technologies. Is 14 years too slow? How fast do you want to grow to the size that you circled earlier?

How Much Risk?

My partner and I were risk-averse. We moonlighted and bootstrapped the start-up of our plastics business for two years while we kept our day jobs.

We continued moonlighting for another year until we were reasonably certain that we would succeed. Our total risk exposure was $15,000. It took us three years to go into our business full time, but we minimized the risk of failure and minimized our financial exposure. What risk tolerance do you have for potential losses?

How about the Future?

Do you envision building a small, comfortable lifestyle company and running it for the foreseeable future, or would you strive to grow a high-potential venture quickly, selling your company within five to 10 years?

What do these four *hows* have to do with opportunity recognition and screening? Simply this: If you would feel successful building a small business slowly (for starters), make a commitment to yourself *right now* that you will go for it. Commit a small sum of money to test your screened opportunity. Don't risk a major amount of capital. You will know soon whether you are on the scent of a real opportunity. Isn't this the most definitive of all screening techniques? Let the success itself be the proof. But don't quit your day job until you know. So many entrepreneurs get frozen in the headlights like deer in the middle of the road. They get too analytical about ideas and opportunities, to the point of inaction. If you can't know for certain, but your gut says GO and the potential loss will be small, GO FOR IT. Personally, I am like Ed and Mellanie. I rely on my gut feeling and passion. I prefer less thinking and more action. My mindset is to take one rapid frugal step in the most likely direction, and to evaluate whether another quick parsimonious step should be taken. At some point soon, I will have my go/no-go answer without spending much money.

On the other hand, if success to you means growing a large company quickly, the risk factors can become very significant. You need to be thorough and analytical in your approach to opportunity recognition. Look at the relationships between size, growth rate, risk, and capital needs in the Figure 6.3. This four-box matrix indicates that both risk and capital requirements increase dramatically when you seek to grow a high-potential venture quickly. This is the scenario that venture capital investors seek. They want to invest in high-potential ventures that grow rapidly and that can be harvested (sold, taken public, or merged) within a five-to 10-year time frame.

Types of companies that fit into the rapid growth, high-potential track are Compaq Computer, Staples, and Home Depot, to name a few. With astute decisions, hard work, and some luck, your business may someday join this list of prestigious companies.

Figure 6.3 Business Size, Growth Rate, Risk, Capital Needs

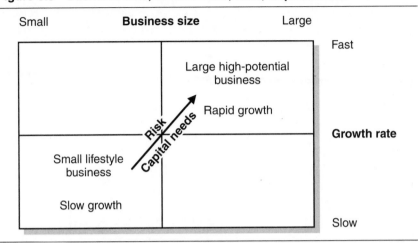

Source: www.CompetitiveSuccess.com, "Business Size, Growth Rate, Risk, Capital Needs." Copyright © 2005 by Michael E. Gordon. Used with permission.

SUMMARY

There is a world of difference between an idea and an opportunity. This chapter describes the nine screening categories to test the difference. Those ideas that emerge from the Opportunity Screening Funnel have the greatest likelihood of turning into profitable Money Machines. Four possible scenarios can befall your business: two nonsuccesses and two successes (Figure 6.1). As you gain proficiency with the funnel, your chance of success will increase.

Actions

√ If you have an idea that feels right after you have squeezed it through the Opportunity Screening Checklist, go for it! Commit a small amount of capital to test the opportunity further. Don't stay frozen in the headlights.

√ If your idea-opportunity plate is empty, go back to Chapter 5 and continue to fill the funnel proactively.

7

BOOTSTRAP

In this chapter, you learn about bootstrapping, the most expedient and least risky path to launching and growing your business with limited financial resources. Bootstrapping is one of the great visual words in the English language. Imagine pulling yourself up *off the ground* by the straps of your own boots, resulting in your upward trajectory in defiance of gravity. Seems impossible? And yet, that is often the best way to get started and to grow your business. I, along with countless other entrepreneurs, have bootstrapped. Bootstrapping is the process of conserving financial resources to the extreme, mostly doing the needed tasks yourself, to get your business up and running.

THE BOOTSTRAPPING OF PLASTECHNOLOGY

In the previous chapter, Mark Greene and Larry Quinn were riddled with indecision. Is Plastechnology an opportunity? If so, what were their next steps? Which of the 4 scenarios actually played out? Here's what happened. You may have already guessed that I was Mark Greene and my real partner, Len Cohen, was given the pseudonym of Larry Quinn. Plastechnology was the case study of the actual startup of our injection-molding company. Len and I were trying to decide whether to buy the equipment at the upcoming auction. It was not an easy decision because the machinery was old, dismantled, too large, and not congruent with our vision. But we believed in ourselves, we believed in the opportunity, and the equipment was affordable. We had faith that we could adapt to the marketplace. All we needed was a start. So we made up our minds to go for it and bought the injection-molding equipment the next day. We pooled $15,000 from our personal savings. Our next decision shaped the course of our lives for the coming two years. We were resolved to build an operating factory using only our initial investment of $15,000, which included the $6,500 cost of the equipment. It seemed like an impossible goal, but we became master bootstrappers. We fought negative cash flow, dollar by dollar.

There were four reasons for our bootstrapping approach:

1. We simply did not have the financial resources to go first class. First class meant hiring others to do what had to be done. In the absence of money, we did everything we possibly could ourselves.
2. We did not want to take on further debt or negative cash flow before we knew that we had a real opportunity. We both had mortgages and limited financial reserves.
3. Later on, even when we did have sufficient capital, the process of watching cash flow closely forced us to be creative, cost-efficient, and focused on the essential priorities.
4. Because we did not want to sell equity and have other partners, we owned 100 percent of the business when we finally sold it.

There were downsides to our bootstrapping approach, however:

- Having too few financial resources often caused wrong decisions to be made. We often did tasks that, in the long run, could have been done cheaper, better and faster by specialists.
- Bootstrapping often limited what might have been more rapid growth. For example, we designed our own marketing literature and built our own trade show booth. This lack of professionalism certainly sent a negative impression of the company to potential customers.
- Our bootstrapping gave resource-rich competition a head start. Competitors with deeper pockets were able to spend money freely on advertising, product development, and state-of-the art equipment. Sometimes we just didn't have a choice; we did what we could do.

We located our factory-to-be in the boiler room of the defunct Tadcaster Brewery in Worcester, Massachusetts. The rent was free, except that we needed to absorb all costs for leasehold improvements. The space had previously been used as an industrial rag storage warehouse. The roof leaked and the smell of rotting rags and old beer hops permeated the air. To call it a mess would have flattered its condition. But we didn't have to pay a monthly lease, saving us cash. Undaunted, we set about developing a state-of-the-art factory. We had a concrete floor poured, and had the machines rigged into our factory according to the floor plan we designed. An electrical contractor brought power to the machines. For two years we worked at our plant evenings and weekends while we kept our day jobs. The reason for the day jobs was that we had homes, families, mortgages, dogs, and a quality of life that we were not willing to put at risk. There were great sacrifices during the start-up phase, but the exhilaration more than made up for any personal deprivation.

Whatever we could do ourselves, we learned and did. Not only did we assemble and rebuild the three molding machines, but we hung lights from the 20-foot ceiling, installed the gas heating system, painted the brick walls, repaired the roof, rebuilt the doors, built storage racks, and on and on (Figures 7.1 through 7.6). After two years, we had an operating factory. We hired a manager, who doubled as a molding technician, to run the

Figure 7.1   Mike, Covered with Paint and Grease, with Our Advisor, Morris Wolfson

Photo courtesy of Michael E. Gordon, 1985.

Figure 7.2 Mike Rebuilding. If You Think You Can, You Will!

Photo courtesy of Michael E. Gordon, 1985.

Figure 7.3 Len Beautifying Our Factory

Photo courtesy of Michael E. Gordon, 1985.

Figure 7.4   Our "State-of-the-Art" Factory

Photo courtesy of Michael E. Gordon, 1985.

Figure 7.5   Len and Mike: Happiness Is Being Your Own Boss!

Photo courtesy of Michael E. Gordon, 1985.

Figure 7.6   You Never Know Where Those Small Steps Will Lead

Photo courtesy of Michael E. Gordon, 1985.

factory in our absence. And when our factory was up and running, there remained in our bank account . . . $550! Can you imagine our excitement when the molding machines began to produce plastic parts?

Shortly thereafter, one of us went into the company full time (revenues were about $40,000 at that time and the other partner joined full time when sales reached about $100,000). And what was the net result? We committed a fixed amount of risk capital; we took it step by step; we bootstrapped to conserve every dollar; and we took the final risk in stages only when we had confidence that our chance of success was high. At any stage of the process, we could have pulled the plug and recovered. There was never a point that our losses would have sunk us.

Isn't this do-it-yourself model worth considering for the start-up and growth of your own venture? There are other approaches, but ours had maximum flexibility with minimal financial risk. Other approaches would have required us to commit to collateralized loans or to have investment partners, neither of which we wanted.

The photographs in Figures 7.1 through 7.5 represent our bootstrapping activities over the two-year start-up period. From these very humble beginnings, our business became quite successful (Figure 7.6).

If you think our bootstrapping odyssey was unique, let me share two other tales with you.

Nicholas Graham

Nicholas Graham had the idea to make neckties from dramatic fabrics. In 1981, at the age of 24, he began buying unusual bolts of cloth and sewing them into neckties on a sheet of plywood in his home. Bootstrapping each step of the way, he personally would select the materials, sew the product, and go around making sales. The money he collected was immediately used to buy more fabrics. Two years later, at the suggestion of a Macy's buyer, Nicholas began using his interesting fabrics to make underwear. In his first year in the underwear business, he generated sales of $600,000. By 1991, revenues were $22 million. Today, the Joe Boxer company has a full line of apparel, accessories and items for the entire family and is a wholly owned subsidiary of the publicly traded company Iconix Brand Group (ICON). Not bad for a young bootstrapping musician-turned-entrepreneur![1]

Jack Doherty

Jack Doherty[2] did not start small. In his own words, "I started smaller than small. I love T-shirts and what they allow people to do. They open up lines of communication." At 18 years old, in pursuit of his passion, he began to bootstrap the start-up of his screen printing T-shirt business in his mother's basement. "My first shirt was NO FUN ALLOWED WESTFIELD STATE. I sold hundreds. It was a blast. I gave out a few shirts to the good-looking girls and the football stars, therefore making it easy to sell them. My second shirt was about graduation: THE PARTY IS OVER NOW WHAT DO WE DO!" After years of coming up with ideas and doing the screen printing himself, part time, he made the jump to full time in 1996. "I set up a showroom and office in a triple-decker in Dorchester, and paid my artist $5 per hour, but I wasn't able to take a draw! Ugh." Today, his company, College Hype, has six offices, two showrooms, many registered trademarks and copyrights, and a loyal following of customers, including the Boston Red Sox Foundation and all of the Curt Schilling Charities. Not bad for an 18-year-old T-shirt-loving bootstrapper!

Bootstrapping is not only for the cash-strapped entrepreneur, but for anyone who wants to accomplish the maximum for the minimum cost. Here is the tabulation of what bootstrappers do:[3]

- They work exceptionally long hours.
- They cut way back on personal expenses to conserve money for their business.
- They often keep their full-time jobs.
- They personally do all the chores needed to build the business—absolutely everything, including manufacturing, packaging, shipping, receiving, cleaning, selling, answering the phones, developing the marketing literature, handing out flyers, purchasing, sleuthing competitors, performing market surveys, visiting customers, responding to the customers days, nights, and weekends.
- They seek advance payments for products to be delivered.
- They brainstorm with teammates, advisors, and friends to solve problems, make decisions, and generate creative ideas to save cash.
- They take internships to learn about an industry from the inside.
- They mobilize free resources.
- They think BIG, but they spend small.
- They barter for almost everything.
- They refuse to be stopped just because they don't have money.

So, how can you become a first-class master bootstrapper? Develop a complete list of all labor, services, equipment, and materials that you require to accomplish your priority milestones. Then brainstorm with creative accomplices to determine how you can minimize costs, even to the level of zero, if at all possible. Your objective is to trade your time, imagination, and effort for the money you don't have. This in no way implies that you will settle for low-quality, ineffective marketing, or long lead times to accomplish needed tasks.

Use the Bootstrapper's Checklist (Exhibit 7.1) to help you make decisions to conserve cash in the start-up and growth of your business. Row by row, find ways to minimize cash outflow.

Throughout this book, I encourage you to control cash flow, but don't be penny wise and pound foolish. Do not hesitate to spend money where it will help to communicate your vision and enhance your chance of success.

Downloadable Exhibit 7.1 Bootstrapper's Checklist*

Money Needed For	Brainstorm Ways to Accomplish by Spending Nothing, Using Only Your Labor or Very Minimal Cash	Comments and Priorities
Rent		
Equipment		
Salaries		
Marketing/Advertising		
Sales literature		
Printing		
Product development		
Contract labor		
Advisory services		
Legal services		
Accounting services		
Repairs		
Prototype development		
Inventory		
Painting		
Electrical		
Plumbing		
Others		

SUMMARY

Bootstrapping is the process of conserving financial resources to the extreme, mostly by doing the needed tasks yourself, to get your business up and running. There are reasons for and against bootstrapping. The positives: avoiding the necessity for outside investors and debt; watching cash flow; and minimizing financial risk. The negatives: delaying more rapid growth; consuming time; and making wrong decisions. Sometimes it is the only way to get going.

Actions

√ With your opportunity in hand, crawl through Exhibit 7.1 and devise your own bootstrapping plan to get your venture off the ground with limited financial resources and with minimal risk.

√ Take one small bootstrapped step at a time.

8

PLAN FOR THE WAR WITH
YOUR COMPETITORS

You have identified an entrepreneurial opportunity. Now what? The next step is to find out everything you can about your competition and the industry dynamics. The term *industry dynamics* refers to the commercial exchanges among five competing forces in the marketplace: the bargaining power of buyers, the bargaining power of suppliers, the threat of substitutes, the entry of new competitors, and the rivalry among existing competitors. *It's a jungle out there!* This chapter prepares you for the coming war with your competition and enables you to:

- Apply these five forces (Porter's Five Forces) to your industry.
- Identify *good* and *bad* industries.
- Sleuth and analyze your competitors.
- Become the fiercest competitor in your industry.

PORTER'S FIVE FORCES

What industry forces will you face when you launch and grow your venture? Even though you have identified an opportunity, some industries are too difficult to penetrate. Your opportunity makes sense *only* if it can capture market share and become a positive Money Machine. According to Michael Porter, there are five competing forces that come into play in every industry (see Figure 8.1).[1]

This elegantly simple framework will help you to understand the power balances in the industry you intend to enter. Your competition is only one fifth of the equation. Ask yourself: Who has the power in your marketplace?

- Buyers are the customers for your goods or services.
- Suppliers provide raw materials and other necessary ingredients to industry participants.
- Substitutes are actually competitors by virtue of the fact that they offer different ways to satisfy customer needs.
- Potential entrants represent the threat of new competitors coming into the marketplace.
- Competitive rivalry refers to the intensity of the battle for market share by the existing combatants.

Figure 8.1 The Five Competitive Forces That Determine Industry Profitability

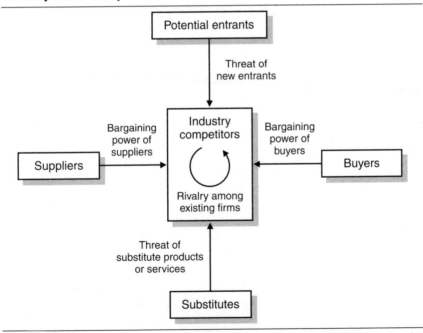

Source: Michael E. Porter, *Competitive Strategy: Techniques for Analyzing Industries and Competitors* (New York: Free Press, 1998), p. 4. Used with permission.

To highlight the principles of this industry framework, I will be referring to examples from our static control company. We were serving the emerging microelectronics industry when the window of opportunity was opening. The use of personal computers was exploding, and embedded smart chips were finding rapid acceptance in appliances and equipment of all kinds. To our good fortune, microelectronic chips, devices, integrated circuits, and systems were susceptible to damage by static electricity. Our company responded to this need by developing, producing, and marketing a line of products that measured and eliminated static electricity for microelectronic equipment makers. Over the years, our company invented and patented several unique static control products that became industry standards.

To illustrate how you can apply Porter's Five Forces model, let's analyze what goes on at an industry trade show, which is a microcosm of the entire industry. Trade shows for the static control and electronics industries were held many times each year in large conference centers around the world. Perhaps 200 to 500 competitors and suppliers would come together to display their products and services to the strolling audience of industry participants. These shows were like huge shark tanks in which buyers, suppliers, new entrants, substitutes, competitors, distributors, and sales representatives were swimming together.

I had mixed emotions about participating in these events. On one hand, it was an opportunity to showcase our new and best products to customers and to potential sales representatives and distributors. On the other hand, every competitor would be studying our offerings to see how quickly they could copy us.

Power of Buyers

In the static control industry, and most industries for that matter, the power was with the largest, most sophisticated buyers and the largest distributors. Not only did they have strong negotiators in their purchasing departments, but they also regulated the quality specifications very tightly. At that time, the dominant buyers were AT&T, Northern Telecom, Analog Devices, Raytheon, and Analogic Corp., to name a few. We were able to make inroads into these large buyers and distributors because we were creating valuable and differentiated products that were temporarily unavailable from our competitors. However, we knew that those competitors would rapidly try to copy our creations. You can imagine what happened to our profit margins when large buyers had more power than suppliers and competitors. Our profits on commodity products were squeezed, but our margins on our unique products remained attractive.

Power of Suppliers

Certain products, such as static-dissipative table tops, fabrics, flooring, carpeting, shoes, and tote boxes were controlled by a limited number of primary suppliers. Suppliers had the power over these products because of the capital-intensive nature of their manufacturing processes and the limited number of suppliers in the static control business at that time. These large suppliers could control who had access to their products as well as the pricing. They could decide to sell through distributors, or to take orders directly from the end customer.

Threat of New Entrants

We were in a highly competitive industry. Even though we had patents on several of these products, it was not possible to keep competitors out. Our success depended on our ability to develop new products and to capture market share quickly, product by product. On occasion, our suppliers, distributors, and even ex-employees became our competitors by copying or sourcing substitute products. In general, the barriers for new competitors to enter the static control industry were not very high, particularly if they had a sales/marketing background in that industry. By knowing the customers' buying requirements and the sources of supply for static control materials, new entrants could come in without high capital requirements.

Substitutes

Substitute products offer different solutions to satisfy the customers' needs. By way of example, we had a patent on a static-protective garment. Suddenly, we observed that one of our competitors was "copying" this product. Subsequently, we learned that they were using a technology that wasn't covered by our patent. Theirs was a substitute for our product, and it did the job. Conversely, we invented new products, some of which were substitutes for our competitors' products. For example, we developed a static-dissipative floor finish as an alternative to static-dissipative floor tiles. Our product solved the problem of static control without the need for customers to replace their existing flooring.

Intensity of Competitive Rivalry

We were engaged in battle with our competitors. Every day, week, month, year, our competitors were thinking (or should have been thinking) how to take market share from us; how to win purchase orders; how to copy our products and services; how to take our best ideas and use them against us (best practices); how to lure our key customers and employees away from us. In fact, they had a responsibility to their stakeholders to achieve competitive advantages at our expense.

What are the consequences for your company when your industry has intense competition? Price wars, nasty competitor behavior, and thin profit margins. As I mentioned, patents don't necessarily keep competitors out of the market. One of our more aggressive competitors copied our patented products, even to the point of including our engineering mistakes. We tried to keep control of our products, but to no avail. Determined competitors like this one know that most companies will avoid costly litigation if at all possible, even if it means not contesting patent infringements.

GOOD AND BAD INDUSTRIES

Based on the opportunity you identified, you will be competing in a *good*, a *marginal*, or *bad* industry. Some industries are more favorable than others. It is to your advantage to understand what characterizes good and bad industries,[2] and to factor that understanding into your decision to start a business in that particular industry.

One way to size up the potential of an industry is to understand where it is in its life cycle. All industries go through a cycle of life—from birth, to youth, to growth, to maturity, to decline, as shown in Figure 8.2. Good industries are found between the emergence and flattening segments of the curve. Bad industries are between maturity and decline.

If you are not yet in the marketplace and your industry is stagnant, you must take market share from your existing competition. This is tough. Vi-

Figure 8.2   Industry Life Cycle

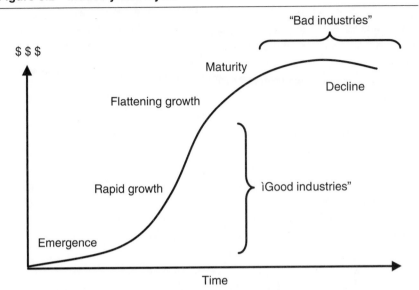

sualize a pie. All of the existing competitors already have carved the pie into different sized slices. You must capture your share by taking from them. This is where strategy and competitive advantages come into play (Chapter 12).

In a growing industry, you can be pulled up with the expansion of the market itself. A rising tide raises all boats, and the boats that add the greatest value for the customer rise fastest.

Having started businesses at both ends of the industry spectrum—good and bad—I now appreciate the importance of being in a good industry, to the extent possible. Regarding our static-control business, recall that the microelectronics industry was entering a rapid growth phase. Simultaneously, it had been determined that microelectronic chips, integrated circuits, and systems were susceptible to damage merely from the *proximity* of electrostatic fields. This opportunity had home-run potential written all over it: a large and rapidly growing microelectronics market, plus a compelling customer need to protect high-valued, static-sensitive products. Furthermore, the methodology for static protection had not stabilized, and there were opportunities for us to invent new products and services.

Our plastics injection-molding business was on the other end of the spectrum. This sector of the plastics industry had already matured. It had been around for more than 50 years and the growth rate was flattening. Although new applications for injection-molded products continually surfaced, there really were no obvious untapped market niches. It was a constant battle to capture customers; rival competitors cut their prices to hold or capture market share. Furthermore, it was becoming easier to source molds and molded products in Asia, Latin America, and Eastern Europe.

A bad industry does not predict failure. It is worth noting that even in a bad industry, certain competitors do better than others, and some even do quite well. For example, the airline industry is fiercely competitive and is subject to high fuel costs and economic ups and downs. Most airlines have been losing money in this environment, yet Southwest Airlines has been remarkably profitable. Herein lies the importance of *knowing everything about all of your competitors* as well as the industry dynamics. That knowledge will give you insights to pursue your own opportunity in a way that can maximize your chance of success and profitability. You can absorb your competitors' best practices.

Is the opportunity you've identified in a good or a bad industry? You can use the checklist in Exhibit 8.1 to find out.

No matter what the nature of your industry, your challenge is to figure out how you will gain competitive advantage. When the customer has choices, why would you be the preferred supplier? (See Chapter 12).

COMPETITOR SLEUTHING

The *Art of War* was written by Sun Tzu, a mysterious Chinese warrior-philosopher, more than 2,000 years ago.[3] His writings teach us to achieve victory over our enemies through *understanding* the opponent's military leadership, organizational efficiency, vulnerabilities, momentum, strengths, and many more parameters. This is competitor sleuthing. The more you know about your competition, the better prepared you will be for the coming never-ending battle. Knowledge is power!

Begin competitor sleuthing by defining your geographic market. This is the actual geographic region in which you will compete. Recall Maria's beading business from Chapter 5. Her business was going to be local, perhaps within a 5- to 10-mile commuting distance of Brookline, Massachusetts. Our plastics injection-molding business was regional; the majority of our customers and competitors were located in New England.

Downloadable Exhibit 8.1   Industry Analysis Checklist*

What You Need to Know	Specific Analysis	Your Conclusions
Growth rate and stage of your industry?	Emerging, rapid growth, flattening, maturing, declining	
Present size of total industry?	If you had every dollar of sales for your product or service, what would your total sales be?	
Is the industry susceptible to disruption?	Are there emerging industry threats?	
Is it a good industry?	Growing, opportunities for new developments: Will you be able to gain market share?	
Is it a bad industry?	Stagnant, dominated by powerful competitors, in decline, impenetrable	
Do you have competitive advantages that can enable market penetration?	Why would buyers do business with you? Are you unique?	
Buyers: Nature of their power?	Do buyers control the industry? How do they exert control?	
Suppliers: Their power?	Do suppliers control the industry? How do they exert control?	
Substitutes: Who are they?	Are there substitute products that you have not considered?	
New Entrants: Who are they?	Who else might come into this industry and disrupt the balance?	
Can you gain sales and market share?	If you cannot capture customers on an increasing basis, the industry may be unfavorable, or your products may be lacking.	
Other specifics to your industry?		

The geographic market for our static-control business, in contrast, was global; we had sales representatives and distributors in North America, Europe, and Southeast Asia. My web business, www.AngelDeals.com, is virtual and global.

Once you've defined your geographic market, determine which firms you'll be competing against. For each of these, systematically analyze the following: strengths, weaknesses, strategies, size, market share, similarities and differences of products and services, business designs (how they make money; see Chapter 9), methods of competing, market penetration strategies, customers, and best practices to copy.

There are many ways to obtain that information about your competitors. Here are some that I have found useful:

- *Competitor web sites:* This method is immensely productive; your significant competitors will certainly have web sites. Use a few different search engines, because many of them employ different searching technologies: www.Yahoo.com, www.google.com, www.ask.com. Also, use many different search terms for each search engine. By way of example, in my web business, www.AngelDeals.com, our mission is "Getting Entrepreneurs Funded." To find our competitors, I would use the following search phrases: angel financing, venture funding, finding investors, getting entrepreneurs funded, angel investor networks, venture capital database, directory of venture investors, how entrepreneurs get funded, finding capital providers. If you search for my business using "getting entrepreneurs funded," my site will come up on pages 1 to 6, depending on the search engine you use. When sleuthing your most significant competitors' web sites, print out the major pages and construct a large mosaic on the wall of how visitors move through their site. This tells volumes about their strategies and product offerings.
- *Online data:* While you are on the Web, surf around to other valuable sites. If you want to find out about competitors that are public companies, go to www.bigcharts.com, type in the ticker symbol (which you can find easily on Yahoo Finance: http://finance.yahoo.com/lookup), then look under "Industry." You will find other public companies in the same industry, as well as their performance. Also, you can find all public company filings on www.sec.gov. Furthermore, many companies list announcements on their sites under "Investor Relations."

- *Libraries:* It is easy to overlook libraries because of the convenience of searching the Web. However, I have found the Kirstein Business Branch of the Boston Public Library to be an invaluable industry resource. The reference personnel are extremely helpful, and I always come away with answers when I have asked how I can find all pertinent information about my competitors. Your local library will have invaluable industry resources similar to those listed next.
- *Databases:* Electronic databases are very useful. Reference United States, for example, has a complete directory of businesses according to their SIC codes (Standard Industry Classification). Databases are often available at libraries.
- *Dun and Bradstreet:* This directory is a subscription registry of private companies in all industries. Your library or your bank might give you access.
- *Trade shows:* The schedule for industry trade shows can be found in *Trade Show Week Data Book* by Trade Show Week, and also in *Trade Show World* by Thompson Gale (find these at your library). Trade shows are my favorite approach to understanding the interactions of all of Porter's Five Forces. Recently, in support of a client, I visited the Iron and Steel Technology Conference and Exposition in Cleveland. Within five hours, I had talked to 50 companies and took home eight pounds of literature from suppliers, buyers, competitors, substitutes, and potential new entrants. This was a crash course in the steel industry.
- *Franchising information:* If your competitors are franchisees, you can find invaluable specific information on how they do business. I call your attention to *Franchising Opportunities Guide* by the International Franchising Association and also the *Ultimate Book of Low Cost Franchises* by *Entrepreneur Magazine.* If you are growing a food business, for example, search for a franchisor of similar nature in your geographic market and study the franchising materials (if available).
- *Yellow Pages:* www.yellowpages.com and the hard copy are invaluable resources to find competitors.
- *Trade magazines:* Industry-specific magazines have a wealth of current information. These are often available at your library.
- *Miscellaneous:* Walk around, talk to customers in your geographic market. Buy competitors' products and analyze their strengths and weaknesses. Talk to your competitors (you might be surprised what they will tell you after one beer).

You'll discover many more sources of competitor information as you begin to dig. Open one door and you're likely to find more doors. Avoid surprises by setting yourself the goal of defining ALL of your major competitors, substitutes, buyers, and future entrants in your Geographic Market (GM). If you don't find them all beforehand, they will certainly show up later, at a most unpleasant time. One way to summarize the information you uncover is to use a form similar to the one shown in Exhibit 8.2.

BECOME THE FIERCEST COMPETITOR

The information you have already gathered (Exhibit 8.2) will lead you to become the fiercest competitor in your GM. Select the best bits and pieces from each of your competitors. Borrow their best practices shamelessly! Assemble the bits together into a composite profile of the ideal unbeatable competitor to emulate. Now for the home run: Do their best even better—offer unparalleled customer service, add greater value for the customer, market more intensely, outsell them more relentlessly, try harder, run faster.[4]

SUMMARY

Your business will fit into an industry where five forces will be interacting: buyers, suppliers, substitutes, future entrants, and competitors. This marketplace will either be favorable to your arrival or unfavorable, and it is important to know this in advance. However, even in unfavorable industries, some competitors will do better than others. You will benefit from becoming a clever sleuth and learning everything you can about your competition. By selecting the best features from each of your competitors, you can become the fiercest competitor of the pack.

Actions

√ Choose the best features from many competitors and put them together as your ideal. This is your role model.
√ Don't leave this chapter until you know your industry dynamics: Porter's Five Forces and the goodness or badness of your industry.
√ If the competitor dynamics appear to be unfavorable, ask yourself what you can do with your opportunity: abandon, modify, or continue anyway? If most signals are positive, go for it!

Downloadable Exhibit 8.2   Competitor Analysis*

Your Specific Competitors	Competitor A	Competitor B	Competitor C
Total size (sales, employees)			
Locations (define all, including sales and number of employees at each location)			
Describe ALL important features of each product or service similar to yours			
Which features are most desirable and differentiated?			
Guesstimate their product costs and pricing structure			
Percent of market share?			
Their overall strategy?			
How do they make money?			
The design of their business?			
How they capture customers?			
Strengths?			
Are they gaining strength? Why?			
Weaknesses?			
Are they weakening? Why?			
How do they compete?			
Who are their main customers?			
Their best practices to copy?			
Others?			

9

DESIGN YOUR
MONEY MACHINE

Every entrepreneur makes mistakes, and I am no exception. Some of my false starts can be traced to my lack of focus on the design options for the Money Machine I was creating. In retrospect, I would have done well to ask "What is my best approach to delivering unique value to customers and making the most money?" I've learned my lesson; those unsuccessful attempts were costly and time-consuming. I now put great emphasis on business design options, and that sometimes includes the decision, on careful consideration, not to pursue what at first appears to be a compelling opportunity. This chapter shares the lessons I learned about business design (also known as business modeling) from the vantage point of my involvement in different companies.

**Business design options are the different paths
you might choose in converting your opportunity
into customer satisfaction and sustained profitability.**

BUSINESS DESIGN AND YOUR MONEY MACHINE

Some options will be more profitable, make earning money easier, will lead to competitive advantages and market penetration, will give your business a higher future value, and will be more suited to your abilities. Look at the Money Machine in Figure 9.1. It is a visual representation of the entrepreneurial process from Opportunity to Customer Satisfaction—and money! The metaphor of the machine implies that there is a continuous flow to the process. Each one of your ensuing opportunities feeds into the hopper and is fueled by resources created from those before. It is a never-ending growth cycle.

Inside the machine, all required business functions are inter-acting and churning to deliver goods and services to your customer. The elements relating specifically to business design encompass three

Figure 9.1   Money Machine

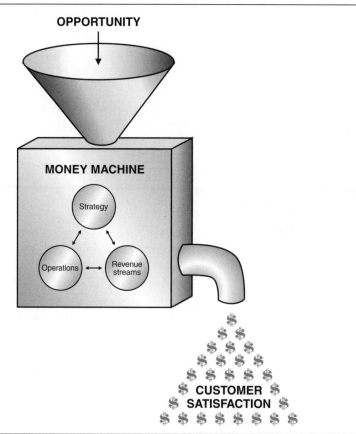

Source: www.CompetitiveSuccess.com, "Money Machine." Copyright © 2000 by Michael E. Gordon. Used with permission.

Figure 9.2 Three Elements of Business Design

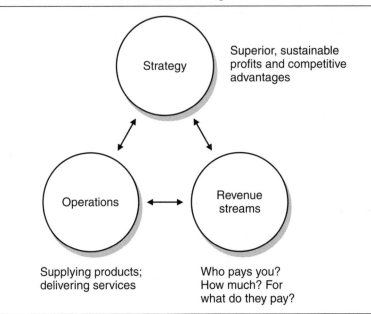

interactive components: Strategy, Operations, and Revenue streams, as shown in Figure 9.2.

THE THREE ELEMENTS OF BUSINESS DESIGN

Strategy

Strategy seeks to gain competitive advantages by differentiating the firm from its competitors. The goal is to accomplish superior, sustainable revenues and profits. What differentiates Domino's Pizza from the hundreds of thousands of other pizzerias? Strategy! Domino's opens pizzerias near colleges and military bases and in busy urban and suburban locations; they deliver hot pizza within 30 minutes; and they build momentum through a network of franchisees. And that is the difference between a $300,000 local pizzeria and a multibillion-dollar global corporation. (Approaches to strategy will be discussed in Chapter 12.)

Revenue Streams

Revenue streams can be another element of differentiation. Who pays you, how much do they pay, for what do they pay, for what else might they pay? By way of example, what distinguishes Bright Horizon's from other child day care facilities? Their recurring revenue streams! Instead of charging parents, it chose to charge corporations that want to offer in-house child care as an attractive benefit for working parents. Bright Horizon's sets up child care centers using the space and facilities of their paying corporate clients. And that is the difference between the average child care business doing $200,000 and Bright Horizon's doing $500 million per year.

Operations

Operations, the method by which you choose to deliver your product or service, is another business design option. What differentiates Wal-Mart, a $350 billion business, from its undersized competitors? Supreme operational efficiency, which translates into the absolute lowest pricing for the customer. And herein lies the importance of business design. Thoughtful consideration and innovation regarding all options of strategy, revenue streams, and operations can lead to huge rewards.

Put these three circles inside the machine, and you have the basis for business design options. A good starting point is to understand what your competitors are doing, and copy their best design options. You might select an ingenious strategy from Competitor A, operational elegance from Competitor B, and sustainable revenue streams from Competitor C. The more astute your selections, the greater the chance and magnitude of success. (This powerful concept of absorbing your competitors' best practices is emphasized throughout the book.)

Many entrepreneurs have done extremely well for themselves by using astute business design. Consider Pierre Omidyar, founder of eBay. He believed that money could be made by connecting people who had items to sell with people who were looking for items to buy, over the Web. The idea was incredibly simple. Other people had set up flea markets, yard sales, and classified ads to bring these buyers and sellers together. But Omidyar modernized the idea, conceiving of an online auction where these transactions could take place anywhere in the world by anyone with an Internet connection. In 1995, he prototyped his idea for a direct person-to-person auction on his own computer and launched his new company using free

Web space and operating out of his apartment. Every time a transaction took place, Omidyar collected a small fee. The design was uncomplicated but powerful, and Omidyar's Money Machine grew explosively over a 10-year period, generating sales in excess of $4.5 billion in 2005.

The business design of Omidyar's venture at startup in 1995 was quite straightforward:

- *Strategy:* eBay connects buyers and sellers of personal items over the Internet. Participants reach agreement on price through the mechanism of a virtual auction. eBay had first-mover advantage in 1995 because the World Wide Web was so new.
- *Revenue streams:* Initially only sellers paid a small fee to list their products for sale. Now eBay also offers myriad products for sale, not at auction.
- *Operational features:* Because it is a virtual connection mechanism, eBay goes to great lengths to ensure the trustworthiness of sellers. Other operational features: simplicity of site design, flawless navigation, and user-friendly customer-facing pages.

What other business design options could eBay have implemented on start-up? Consider Craigslist (www.craigslist.com). It also connects buyers and sellers of products, *as well as services,* over the Internet. In addition, it offers connections for jobs, personals, discussion forums, community involvement, housing, and more. Craigslist serves more than 200 cities around the world. At this time, its revenue stream comes only from employers offering jobs; all other connections are free. Its apparent goal is to build traffic and momentum before implementing other revenue streams. Today, traffic is huge, tens of millions of unique visitors per month, and the company is rapidly displacing and disrupting classified advertising sections of newspapers.

The point of this comparison between eBay and Craigslist is to highlight the concept of business design options. Both companies connect buyers and sellers of personal goods over the Internet. One became a $4.5 billion company in 10 years; the other (apparently) has not yet achieved substantial revenues. *But Craigslist has achieved significant traffic!* As I perceive the situation, the problem Craigslist had was this: If they tried to connect buyers and sellers over the Internet via an online auction, they would face an established 800-pound gorilla: eBay. Most likely, they would have failed. "Let's go the back door route," they might have strategized. "No revenue model at start-up; let's build traffic. If we succeed in this strategy, the traffic will eventually turn into revenue streams." Craigslist penetrated one city at a time, starting with San Francisco, and has built a global people-connection model.

In the face of overwhelming competition, Craigslist's choice of business design was a resounding success.

THREE EXAMPLES AND LESSONS LEARNED

Let's explore business design options in greater depth using three of my business involvements:

1. The family-owned wholesale and retail meat business.
2. The plastics injection-molding company.
3. The static control company that developed and manufactured products for the microelectronics industry.

Meat

The family meat business helped to shape my attitudes about profitability, labor intensiveness, and competitive advantage. As I mentioned earlier, my father wanted me to learn the business from the ground up. Consequently, I worked part time in both the wholesale and retail businesses during high school and college. I loaded and unloaded trucks, put up and delivered orders, organized the freezers, raked meat and debris from the sawdust-covered floors, worked on the boning bench, ground hamburger, steam-cleaned the equipment, and served retail customers. Over the years, I came to appreciate my father's approach to my business education. He wanted me to really understand the challenges of running the wholesale and retail meat operations of the company. And those operations were really intensive. He made sure that I was also exposed to the higher-level strategic issues, the people issues, the opportunities, and competitive threats through discussions around the dinner table over many years.

The wholesale company grew to become a substantial distributor of meats and dairy products to restaurants and supermarkets in the northeastern United States. However, the profit margins were paper thin. The company was vulnerable to changing industry forces, and finally, it went into terminal bankruptcy after 55 years of doing business. The retail outlet still exists today.

Business Design Lessons Learned

- Shun businesses with low profit margins that require extensive human efforts to produce commodity products and services.
- If you are already in a commoditized business, seek to develop competitive advantages through branding of unique value-added products or services.
- Diversify into more profitable industries that would benefit from your company's core capabilities.

Plastics

In flagrant disregard of the lessons learned in the meat business, my partner and I built a plastics injection-molding factory from the ground up. I was again in a mature industry characterized by low profit margins and little opportunity for competitive advantage. We believed there was an opportunity to provide precision, custom injection-molded plastic parts for demanding applications. So the first thing we did was to buy old molding machines and bootstrap the start-up of a plastics factory over a two-year period, evenings and weekends (Option 1). We were not thoughtful about other possible choices. Based on more thoughtful considerations, here is our range of business design options:

Option 1: Buy old molding machines and bootstrap the start-up of a plastics factory over a two-year period, evenings and weekends.

Option 2: Buy one new state-of-the-art, precision molding machine initially, to do prototype development and short production runs. Outsource higher volume jobs.

Option 3: Acquire an injection-molding company.

Option 4: Act as consultants for the industry, particularly for difficult-to-produce applications requiring tool design, material selection, and process control.

Option 5: Same as Option 4, but we could then take orders for molding contracts and outsource the production to domestic, Latin American, and Asian molding companies.

Option 6: Lease time from other plastic factories that were not busy round the clock.

Let's consider these design options in greater detail (Exhibit 9.1).

Downloadable Exhibit 9.1 Business Design Options*

Options Yes/No/?	Converting Opportunity into Money	Analysis of Options
Option 1 ?	Build an injection-molding factory from the ground up by boot-strapping for two years to conserve cash. Buy unproductive, older equipment at auction.	We chose this route because we had limited financial resources. We also were not sure that there was truly an opportunity. Although we succeeded, it was not our best option. Misguided strategy, complex operations, and least profitability.
Option 2 Y	Buy, lease, or finance one new state-of-the-art, small precision molding machine to do prototype development and short molding runs. Outsource higher volume production runs.	This would have been a much-preferred route for us to have taken. We could have financed one new machine and boot-strapped the start-up from that point. We also could have kept our day jobs while we were gaining experience and sales. The financial risk was greater than for Option 1; the time quicker.
Option 3 N	Acquire an injection molding company.	This was not an attractive option because there were few plastics factories near us. We would have had to relocate our families.
Option 4 ?	Act as consultants for the industry, particularly for difficult-to-produce applications requiring tool design, material selection, and process control.	This could have been an option, except it did not fit with our desire to be significant players in the plastics industry. As consultants, our potential for wealth seemed limited. But we could have started this way.
Option 5 Y	Act as consultants for the industry as in Option 4. Take orders for molding contracts and outsource to domestic or foreign companies.	This was our second most attractive option because it would have allowed us to gain momentum before we committed to purchasing equipment and building a factory. It was also the most scalable, in that we would never be limited by the amount we could produce.
Option 6 N	Don't own a factory. Lease time from another plastics factory that has excess capacity.	This would have been difficult to accomplish. Established factories prefer to handle the entire molding job.
Other options		

Source: www.CompetitiveSuccess.com, "Business Design Options." Copyright © 2005 by Michael E. Gordon. Used with permission. ***A blank version of this page can be downloaded from www.trumpuniversity.com/entrepreneurship101 for your personal use.***

So, we had six options from which to choose. But because of our impetuousness, we jumped into Option 1: the most difficult to start, the most operationally intensive, the least potential for competitive advantages, and the least profitable. Bootstrapping a plastics molding factory with out-of-date, unproductive, dismantled molding equipment was not our best option.

Fortunately, the universe sometimes conspires to protect the naive. We did succeed in our injection-molding business. We found three ways to be profitable. First, we focused on customers with technically demanding applications that other molders would have trouble satisfying. These applications included close tolerance, miniature parts, and unique materials (electrically conductive plastics, optical materials, specialty compounded plastics). Second, we sought prototype development work and short molding runs. It was our belief that these short runs would grow into longer production runs, and they often did. Third, we would often "productize" this custom service by molding amounts in excess of the current order. This was a risk if our customers did not place future orders. But if they did, their molded products would be taken from our inventory, and we would have avoided costly machine setup time and process losses. So even in a highly competitive industry, it is possible to devise ways to increase profitability.

Business Design Lessons Learned

- Before you launch your venture, carefully examine ALL business design options to accomplish your vision.
- Select the one option that *fits* you best from the standpoint of profits and your personal objectives, passions, and tolerance for risk.
- Even in a mature, highly competitive industry, you can invent new ways to make money and increase profitability.

Static Control

The static control business was a different animal completely. In our plastics factory, we were doing custom manufacturing for Northern Telecom, Summagraphics, Data General, Kodak, C&K Components, and the like. Many of these companies asked us to mold electrically conductive materials that would dissipate static electricity to prevent damage to their microchips. We could see this segment of our molding business growing, and we began to look for other applications for static-dissipative materials. As we came to understand the needs of the microelectronics industry, we began to invent our own products. We found our strengths in product development and innovation, and we introduced several static control products that became industry standards. Our gross profit margins soared accordingly to 60 percent and even higher in some years. By way of comparison, this gross margin is in the same ballpark as that of Cisco Systems.

Business Design Lessons Learned
- Jump into a rapidly growing industry at the right time.
- Use your skills and competencies to create uniquely valued products or services for your customers. Attractive profits will likely follow.
- A product-oriented business has greater potential for scalability and growth, especially if you can create a branded identity.

SUMMARY

The Money Machine is a visual representation of the entrepreneurial process, from Opportunity to Customer Satisfaction and profitability. Inside the machine, all required business functions are interacting to deliver goods and services to your customer. The elements relating specifically to business design encompass three interactive components: strategy, operations, and revenue streams. The largest payoffs derive from careful analysis of your competitors' business designs, and then innovating beyond them.

Actions

√ After analyzing the business designs of your competitors, select an ingenious strategy from Competitor A, operational elegance from Competitor B, and sustainable revenue streams from Competitor C.
√ Then, go beyond. Innovate!

TRUMP UNIVERSITY
We Teach Success.

Michael Sexton, president of Trump University (www.trumpuniversity
.com), describes the birthing of Trump University. He had been studying the online education market and came to understand the acute
need for virtual continuing studies. "Too few people have an opportunity in life to get an MBA from a prestigious university," he reasoned.
"The need is most acute for those people that don't have the time or
the financial means." His concept was to package the best speakers,
educators, and industry experts and to deliver a variety of hard-
hitting, action-oriented programs over the Web. Though his customers would not receive a degree, they would learn *how to succeed*
from the best coaches. As he studied the economics, the key to success was brand leverage to make this revenue model profitable. The
Trump brand! Michael began to validate his concept through extensive research on the competition, the industry dynamics, the size and
growth rate of the market, positioning and market penetration strategies, and most important—financial projections. After developing an
executive summary, he made contact with the Trump Organization.
Michael was given 15 minutes to pitch his concept directly to Donald
Trump—informal—no PowerPoint. Donald Trump made the decision
to take the concept to the next level; it passed the "sniff test." Not
only was the concept itself compelling, Donald Trump was sizing up
Michael as a potential executive who could deliver, who could mone-
tize the Trump brand. One month later, he went back in with business
plan in hand. It was a go! In building Trump University, there were
many lessons learned, and particularly the trade-offs: speed to market
versus number of products, build programs or buy, today's technology
versus two years down the road. Michael's approach has been to go
for rapid prototyping and market penetration. "Let the market shape
us in the future."

10

VIRTUALIZE AND
GLOBALIZE

No book on entrepreneurship would be complete without some discussion of the most awesome business design imaginable—and right
at your fingertips: the World Wide Web. Who in his wildest imagination
would have predicted in 1990 that anyone with an Internet connection
could have access to 1 billion people around the globe? Literally 1 billion
people—15 percent of the entire human population is connected! At 15
years old, the Web is still in its infancy. We know that it will continue its
phenomenal growth. We also know that this amazing virtual network allows you to be a player in the same global marketplace as the world's
largest companies.

But being on the Web is insufficient for commercial success. You will
never make a dime unless your business design is right. Even then, you
still won't make money unless you pay attention to your only source of
competitive advantage. (Wait for it!) This chapter provides you with practical approaches to:

- Getting the virtual business design for your Money Machine right
- Making money over the Web
- Fixating on your one source of competitive advantage

The Virtual Business Design for Your Money Machine: Getting It Right

A frustrated entrepreneur asked for my advice. He had developed and patented a proprietary technology to produce coffee bags. Like the tea bag, this product was made to steep in hot water for a few minutes, after which: Voila! A piping-hot cup of gourmet caramel mint dark French roast. Competitor sleuthing had not turned up anything similar. "This appeared to be a solid opportunity," he lamented. "I developed an executive summary (Chapter 15), and launched my web business. My market penetration plan was to sell these specialty coffee bags only over the Internet."

Indeed, the aspiring entrepreneur had developed a product line of 100 unique gourmet coffee flavors. He built an inventory, constructed a web site—www.gourmetcoffeebags.com—had his webmaster submit the site to the major search engines, and opened his web doors for business. But almost no one stopped by, and very few orders were placed. "I am really disappointed," he confided. "My site is attractive and user-friendly; the product is superb and highly differentiated. Pricing per cup is the lowest among all other suppliers of specialty coffees. By all the rules of business strategy, shouldn't I have expected better?"

This story is typical of so many Web entrepreneurs: An opportunity turns to exhilaration turns to disappointment. What went wrong? What went wrong was his lack of focus on business design. Recall that business design encompasses the three elements of operations, revenue streams, and strategy (Chapter 9). Let's look at each element to find the problem (actually, the opportunity in disguise).

Operations

His business would be considered a product e-tailer. When an order is placed over the Web, product is taken from inventory, packaged, and shipped. The operations have all the complexities and requirements of a brick and mortar business: manufacturing, outsourcing, shipping, receiving, administration, management, overhead, and so on—the whole nine yards. The only difference is that payment is collected virtually, in advance, via credit card. *The problem isn't here.*

Revenue Streams

Simple: He made money from the sale of coffee bags. (Perhaps he could also offer a line of related products—mugs, coffee makers, biscotti, and the like.) *The problem isn't here either.*

Strategy

His strategy was based on competing by product differentiation, as well as being the lowest-priced supplier of gourmet coffee. What's wrong with this picture?

When he asked me, "By all the rules of business strategy, shouldn't I have expected better?" My answer to him was that the rules of conventional competitive advantage (Chapter 12) do apply on the Web, and those rules are subsumed under one obvious, fundamental, immutable principle:

Sustainable traffic is THE source of competitive advantage on the Web.

Traffic determines success and nonsuccess for Web-based companies. My suggestion to the aspiring coffee king was to become an *expert* on this key to his success: Traffic!

FIXATE ON TRAFFIC: YOUR ONE SOURCE OF COMPETITIVE ADVANTAGE

How can you build sustainable traffic? Three self-evident rules need to be followed:[1]

1. First-time visitors must be able to find your site easily.
2. Visitors must be completely satisfied with their first experience.
3. Visitors must have strong reasons to return for more, based on your business design.

Let's examine each of these important rules.

First-Time Visitors Must Be Able to Find Your Site Easily

Using the coffee bag example, try this exercise. Assume you are a potential customer for gourmet coffees, and you prefer to buy online because the selection is so broad. You search Google.com, Yahoo.com, and Ask.com for "specialty coffees" and "gourmet coffees." A vast number of sites are found:

Search Engines	Specialty Coffee Sites	Gourmet Coffee Sites
Google.com	1,290,000	805,000
Yahoo.com	963,000	679,000
Ask.com	189,000	276,000

Yes, hundreds of thousands of sites come up when potential customers search for coffees. If you try to narrow the search to "coffee bags," what comes up are paper and foil bags for packaging coffee. I cannot think of any search terms that would do much better. If *your* site does not come up in the first five search-result pages, few potential customers will find you. That is your challenge: to come up in the first five pages of search results. When I performed this coffee search, I noticed that www.bocajava.com came up first on Google.com as well as Ask.com. How did the vendor accomplish this? bocajava.com was buying first page position through Search Pages Ads, to be discussed shortly. When they stopped buying ads, their position dropped.

In addition to conventional (nonweb) advertising, new visitors will find you through seven virtual channels.

1. Search Engine Meta Tagging

Meta tags are the labels that search engines use to find sites. To see the meta tags for bocajava.com, first go to its web site, then right click on the very top of their home page. Then left click on "view source." You will see its meta description and key words: "coffee, expresso, tea, specialty coffee, gourmet coffee, flavored coffee, coffee blends, coffee beans, coffee gifts, coffee sampler, gifts, holiday gifts, specialty gifts, coffee roaster," and many, many more. Essentially, these are the search terms that potential new visitors can use to find this particular site. How can you use meta tagging to your advantage? Search for your primary competitors over the Web and find their meta tags, meta descriptions, and meta labels. Do what they are doing. Choose the best meta tags from all of your competitors' sites; use their collective best practices against them. Your webmaster will then embed these tags into your own site. A wealth of information is available on www.wikipedia.org. More specifically, go to http://en.wikipedia.org/wiki/Meta_tag, as well as http://en.wikipedia.org/wiki/Search_engine_marketing.

2. Reciprocal Links

Reciprocal links are links to and from other web sites that are related to yours in some way. For example, the gourmet coffee vendor might establish reciprocal links with a premium online vendor of biscotti or other foods that complement coffee consumption. Sites that establish reciprocal links share traffic for mutual gain. As an example, go to www.AngelDeals.com. At the bottom, click on "Link Exchange?" Copy our best practices. For further information, see http://en.wikipedia.org/wiki/Reciprocal_link.

3. Search Page Ads

Another way to be found by Web searchers is through pay-per-click advertising. Pay-per-click ads are text ads placed near search results; when a site visitor clicks on the ad, the advertiser is charged a small amount. Google Adwords and Yahoo! Search Marketing are the two largest providers of pay-per-click advertising. To find more information about these effective programs: On the home page of Google.com, left click on "business solutions," then left click on "adwords"; for Yahoo!, on the left navigator bar below "Small Business," left click on "Search Listings," then click on "How Sponsored Search Works," and watch the tutorial.

Pay-per-click ads tend to be expensive. Therefore, this technique works particularly well when the product or service carries a high profit margin. Using bocajava.com as an example, assume that the key ad phrase is "Buy the world's largest selection and finest gourmet coffees from bocajava.com." Here are the assumptions needed to calculate the cost-effectiveness of this pay-per-click advertising program:

- Assume that bocajava.com pays $1 for every visitor who clicks on this ad phrase and is beamed to bocajava.
- Assume further that one out of 50 new visitors will make a purchase.
- Assume that the average sale to one customer is $100.
- Assume that the cost of goods sold is $50.

The bottom line is that bocajava.com paid $50 in advertising dollars to have 50 new visitors and to capture $50 in gross profits. Breakeven! To me that is a winner for two reasons:

1. Many first-time customers will come back for more, with no further advertising costs to bocajava.com.
2. The sales funnel (Chapter 12) can possibly be optimized for greater profitability: number of new visitors, cost of goods sold, average sale to one customer, and size of order.

4. Web Directories

Web directories specialize in linking your site to other web sites and categorizing those links. They allow you to add or submit your own listing, and most of them are free. The most effective directory is www.DMOZ .com (also known as Open Directory Project). Here is how to submit your own directory listing: Go to www.DMOZ.com. On the horizontal navigator bar on the top, left click "Suggest URL." Follow directions from there. I call your attention to www.best-web-directories.com as a valuable source of comparative information about other web directories. For more information, see http://en.wikipedia.org/wiki/Web_directory.

5. Publicity Releases

Also known as press releases, publicity releases are a method of promoting your site free of charge (usually). Hard copy magazines as well as electronic magazines (e-zines) need newsworthy stories, and they will often publish yours if it is compelling. Using the coffee example, search for appropriate magazines using the term "coffee magazines" or "coffee e-zines." A range of magazines will come up for you to pursue. You can then submit your publicity release to each magazine directly. For further information, see http://en.wikipedia.org/wiki/Publicity.

6. Viral Marketing

Viral marketing is a method of word-of-mouth advertising over the Internet. The goal is to create an electronic "tipping point"[2] that spreads your message over the Web at an epidemiclike rate. In essence, your goal is to create buzz through referrals. You can put links on all pages that say "Tell a friend." Look on the bottom of www.AngelDeals.com and you will see "Tell a Colleague." Use this concept on your own site. For a more complete description of this technique, refer to http://en.wikipedia.org/wiki /Viral_marketing.

7. Weblogs

Affectionately known as blogs, weblogs are web sites that allow visitors to post their own news items, comments, photos, and thoughts on any subject. These are free, interactive message boards and personal web pages that you could subtly use to lure visitors to your commercial site. To create your own blog, go to www.blogger.com and left click on the arrow "Create Your Blog Now" and follow the steps. Additionally, go to www.Yahoo.com, click on 360° on the vertical left navigator bar, and then click "Start My Page." For more information, see http://en.wikipedia.org/wiki/Blog.

In the end, *your entrepreneurial imagination* may be the most fruitful approach for finding and creating mechanisms that drive people to your site. Are there new ways to use social networks to reach your target customers creatively? Look at the success of www.myspace.com and Yahoo! groups. For further information on this approach, refer to http://www.gigaom.com/2006/05/29/social-networks-are-the-new-media.

Visitors Must Be Completely Satisfied with Their First Experience

When a new visitor does find your site, you have about 10 seconds to get your message across. In that 10 seconds, the viewer must:

- Have a welcoming visual experience
- Clearly understand the *purpose* of your site
- Be called on to take action

If you pass these three tests, the customer must then experience flawless navigation around your site. And if you pass this test and the customer places an order, you must deliver excellent products and services at favorable prices compared to your competition. By way of example, look at www.trumpuniversity.com. Within 10 seconds, you have a strong and welcoming visual message from Donald Trump. You understand the purpose of Trump University: "We teach Success—in Real Estate, Entrepreneurship, Marketing, Wealth Creation, and Career." You are called to action—to sign up for online courses. The navigation is flawless, and you will have a satisfying learning-by-doing experience. This is evidenced by testimonials from satisfied customers as well as customers who sign up for additional courses.

Visitors Must Have Strong Reasons to Return for More, Based on Your Business Design

Repeat purchases are a must for just about every business. Repeat purchases leverage the upfront costs of building an e-commerce site and helping people find it. Repeat purchases can come from:

- The urgency of the concept (e-mail, search engines, auctions, personals, social networks, sports)
- Cravings for certain products (chocolate, coffee, sweets) or services (online gaming)
- Permission marketing, where visitors opt in to receive communications from your company
- Current content and information (world news reports, stock market newsletters, e-zines)
- Products or services that are consumable and needed or wanted continuously (clothing, beauty products, food)

The most successful sites are those that enjoy frequent repeat visitors: Google (information), eBay (auctions), Yahoo! (e-mail).

The least successful sites have one-time buyers. Even if the buyer is satisfied, there is no continuing reason for him or her to return. Note that you can have a smaller successful web business with no repeat customers simply because the size of the total world market is so large. But repeat traffic certainly makes the magnitude of success greater.

MAKING MONEY OVER THE WEB

I've now explained how you can create traffic on your site and what you must do to encourage customers to return. This section examines some business design options for your Money Machine to make money. There is a range of web revenue models; the major ones are discussed next.

Product E-Tailers

As we saw with www.bocajava.com, product e-tailers use their web sites as shopping carts for their products. There is an operational infrastructure behind the scenes to fulfill the purchase order. The operational infrastructure would encompass inventory control, manufacturing or outsourcing, shipping, customer service, and most functions of nonweb businesses. Typical examples of product e-tailers are www.chocolate.com, www.flowers.com, and www.hats.com, to name but three from millions.

Membership

Membership revenue models permit access to valuable sections of a web site for a fee. By way of example, www.AngelDeals.com provides members with access to databases for global venture capital firms and angel investor networks, the ability to create and post executive summaries online, access to contacts around the world, and business planning content.

Advertising

Revenue from advertising is one of the largest categories of money made on the Web. Look at just about every site and you will see advertisements. Money is made in two ways: (1) An advertiser places an ad on your site and pays you an advertising fee; and (2) Google.com (and others) place ads on your site and pay money every time a visitor clicks on the ad. RImarinas.com has done just that. RImarinas.com connects boat owners with marinas in Rhode Island for the purpose of reserving overnight dockage. Its revenue model is based on the Google AdSense program. For further information on this revenue model, see www.Google.com homepage → Business Solutions → Earn revenue with AdSense → Quick tour.

Service Providers

In this business design, a virtual service is provided for a small service fee. Hotels.com permits you to book hotel rooms, and their company receives a fee for providing this booking service. Other examples are tickets.com, angieslist.com, and register.com.

Connectors

In this business design, buyers and sellers are connected virtually, with a credit card charge to one of the parties. This virtual revenue model is exemplified by eBay.com, Match.com, and monster.com.

Content Providers

In this category are information-rich sites, e-zines, and e-newsletters. Most content sites are free, but if the information is truly unique, current, and hard to find, a fee for access is possible. By way of example, Investor's Business Daily offers eIBD online for a fee (see www.investors.com).

SUMMARY

This chapter seeks to whet your appetite to design your Money Machine using virtual revenue models. Seven points of web strategy were identified:

1. Provide a welcoming visual experience.
2. Define the purpose of your site clearly.
3. Call on the visitor to take action.
4. Ensure that navigation is flawless.
5. Offer robust and current content (if applicable).
6. Deliver excellent products and services at favorable pricing compared to your competition.
7. Promote repeat visitors.

Sustainable traffic is THE source of competitive advantage on the Web.

Action

√ Become an expert on making money on the Web.[3] The rewards are potentially huge. From the humblest beginnings, and the simplest of business designs, eBay now has revenues of $4.5 billion. And how about www.youtube.com? $1.6 billion in 2 years!

11

DO WELL AND
DO GOOD

Does it seem contradictory to talk about socially conscious business design in a book devoted to building a Money Machine? After all, a Money Machine is honed to do battle with aggressive competitors. Not at all! Profitability and social responsibility are not mutually exclusive. In fact, customers prefer to do business with companies that make a positive contribution to society.[1] This presents another business design option: doing well financially *and* doing good for society. It is a business design option with no downside risk. In this brief chapter, we explore what you can do to embed social consciousness into your business—and thrive.

Social consciousness is the awareness of social issues and a willingness and determination to do good for society. Our world is faced with many problems: human abuse, pollution, global warming, endangered species, natural resource consumption, and poverty, to name but a few. The encouraging news is that many in the commercial world are doing something about them. Consider these companies: Grand Circle Travel, Timberland, Green Mountain Coffee Roasters, The Body Shop, Ben & Jerry's, Avon, Hewlett-Packard, Gramen Bank, Eziba, Stonyfield Farm,

The MathWorks, Abbott Laboratories, Cisco Systems, Millipore Corp., British Petroleum, New Balance, GTech, and Genzyme Corporation. What do these companies have in common? All have committed to make social consciousness part of their corporate cultures. One might argue that these are large corporations that can afford to be socially conscious. But the fact is, they are *prospering financially*, in part, because of their social initiatives. *And smaller companies can do the same!*

BUSINESS DESIGN OPTIONS

As you design your business, a number of proven models combining successful commerce and social responsibility are worth considering. Here are just a few.

Create a Strategic Alliance with a Nonprofit

Jeffrey Swartz, CEO of Timberland, did just that. Timberland formed an alliance with City Year, a nonprofit urban Peace Corps. City Year volunteers help in nursing homes and child day care centers, tutor schoolchildren, assist on flood control and construction projects, teach social skills on playing fields and school yards, and perform other community services. Timberland's role is not passive; it does not simply provide financial support. Timberland employees spend time serving in their communities. The Timberland Company is a noteworthy example of a for-profit business that has embedded a socially caring culture within its business. And Swartz is a role model of a young business leader who is using the resources of his company for the benefit of society by partnering with a nonprofit organization. Both organizations are thriving. Since the inception of the alliance in 1989, Timberland's stock has risen from $2 to $27 per share, a multiple of 13. By comparison, the Dow increased by a multiple of 5 during that same time frame.

Make Social Responsibility Part of Your Mission

In 1978, Ben & Jerry's was launched in an old abandoned gas station in Burlington, Vermont, with just $8,000 of start-up capital. Its goal was to make Vermont's finest ice cream. Today, the company generates sales of about $300 million and shares profits with its employees and the community. This company operates with both an economic and a social mission, as described on its web site www.benjerrys.com:

- *Economic mission:* To operate the Company on a sustainable financial basis of profitable growth, increasing value for our stakeholders and expanding opportunities for development and career growth for our employees.
- *Social mission:* To operate the Company in a way that actively recognizes the central role that business plays in society by initiating innovative ways to improve the quality of life locally, nationally, and internationally.

Many companies have lofty ideals baked into their mission statements. But Ben & Jerry's really walks the talk. Its Ben & Jerry's Foundation contributes $1.1 million to causes supporting human needs, justice, children, families, the environment, sustainable agriculture, family farms, and waste management. And the company is thriving.

Eliminate Pollution from Your Operations

People once believed that eliminating pollution from their commercial operations—particularly from manufacturing—was a costly luxury that would reduce profitability and competitiveness. We now know that sound environmental practices actually have the opposite effect: They contribute to profits. Let me cite two examples: 3M and Wal-Mart.

3M has had a Pollution Prevention Program (3P) in place for 31 years. According to its web site, www.3M.com, 3P seeks to eliminate pollution through product reformulation, process modification, equipment redesign, and recycling and reuse of waste materials. The 3P program helps prevent pollution at the source: in products and manufacturing processes. According to the company's calculations, 3P has resulted in over *$1 billion* in cost reductions since the program's inception.

Wal-Mart is also learning the benefits of leaning toward green. This world-spanning retailer, with 5,200 stores and growing, is reducing its energy load and environmental impact by experimenting with wind turbines, photovoltaic shingles, light dimmers, reduced packaging, and reduction of gasoline for delivery trucks. It is also using its buyer muscle to urge factories in China to reduce air pollution. In addition to their positive social impact, Wal-Mart's targeted annual cost savings from these initiatives for 2006 are $300 million.

The lesson from these examples is clear: If you examine every operation in your business, you'll find ways to save energy, reduce pollution and waste, cut greenhouse gases, and produce your products more efficiently. Doing these things will give your venture a positive public image *and* improve profitability. Win-win!

Give Back to Your Community

Enlightened executives have discovered that a healthy business depends on a healthy and vibrant community. They contribute to the vibrancy of their communities through combinations of financial support and charitable work. Rhode Island-based Walco (www.WalcoKIP.com) is one noteworthy example. Its president, Ellis Waldman, has nurtured a charitable companywide culture. As Ellis describes his philosophy, "We are members of many communities, and as such, we live by the 'Golden Rule' and we give back from our hearts." As a company, the Walco team participates in the AIDS Walk and Breast Cancer Walk; they collect food for the Rhode Island Community Food Drive; the company and individuals contribute to the United Way, St. Mary's Home, the American Red Cross, and Hearts in Bloom; they donate blood several times per year. And what do the employees feel? Great pride. And what are the benefits? Low absenteeism and the strong desire to remain part of the Walco culture. Twelve percent of the Walco workforce has been there for over two decades!

Does this make sense for a young business? You may find that financial contributions are difficult or impossible during the challenging start-up and early stages of your venture, when every dime is needed in the business. But as these examples make clear, money isn't the only thing that you and your employees can contribute. And the benefits are enormous.

SUMMARY

Social consciousness is a business design option with no downside. This chapter highlights several approaches that your company might take, from small steps to more pronounced steps. Building a culture around good causes creates a strong, motivated team. It also gives your company a positive reputation with customers, which can lead to greater sales and profits. Start small and watch the magic happen to your workforce *and profits.*

Actions

√ Elicit ideas for social participation from your entire company.
√ Eliminate pollution, reduce waste, and minimize energy use in your operations.
√ Establish an alliance with a nonprofit.
√ Build a company culture that is proud to support social causes.

TRUMP

TRUMP MORTGAGE, LLC

Strategy is about gaining competitive advantages. So how does a new entrant, Trump Mortgage, capture market share quickly in a highly competitive, mature $3 trillion industry? Trump Mortgage has a bold vision to become one of the top 10 providers of home and commercial mortgages. As E. J. Ridings, CEO of Trump Mortgage, describes it, "I knew in my heart and soul that Trump Mortgage can make a difference in this gigantic industry. The financial opportunity is huge—but there is more. Not only will we make money, but it is a humanitarian venture as well. We have created a safe haven where people can get the best deal on a residential or commercial mortgage without worrying about all the hidden clauses." For most people, their home and mortgage are the two biggest commitments they will make in life. Even savvy real estate buyers have trouble wading through the bewildering maze of legalese and fee structure when securing a mortgage: mortgage rates, points, origination fees, commitment fees, underwriting fees, processing fees, prepayment penalties, and very fine print. Trump Mortgage's strategy is grounded on many points of competitive differentiation: leverage of the Trump brand; customer relationships based on integrity, honesty, and no surprises; being the most cost-effective provider of mortgages; partnering; and rapid growth through targeted acquisitions.

12

DEVISE A
WINNING STRATEGY

Instinctively we know how crucial strategy is. It is one of those common words we understand, but can't fully define or implement. Countless books and articles have been written on the subject, and the sheer volume of literature can lead to confusion.[1] The goal of this chapter is to filter through the muddle and take the mystery out of business strategy as we explore:

- The what and why of business strategy
- Basic premises
- Approaches to gaining competitive advantages
- Implementing your strategic plan

As you read this chapter, pause along the way and apply these strategic concepts. Use them in converting your opportunity into a competitive, sustainable Money Machine.

ENTREPRENEURIAL STRATEGY DEFINED

Let's start from the bottom and work backward. What does strategy seek to accomplish? The end result of strategy is SUPERIOR, SUSTAINABLE FINANCIAL PERFORMANCE.

Superior, sustainable financial performance means your business will be healthy and will grow in revenues, profits, and return on equity into the future. No confusion here. The challenge comes from figuring out how to accomplish this objective. Harvard professor Michael Porter, whose books *Competitive Strategy*[2] and *Competitive Advantage*[3] have influenced more entrepreneurs and business executives on this subject than any others, has defined strategy as a "broad formula for how a business is going to compete." Simply stated, strategy boils down to beating your competitors in the battle for share of market and becoming the preferred supplier for products or services. This means continuously capturing purchase orders by satisfying customer needs better than your competition. And this leads to superior, sustainable financial performance by differentiation from your competition. A diagram would be useful to follow this chain (Figure 12.1).

The customer makes choices: Why should I choose supplier A instead of Supplier B, C, or Z? Your job is to give the customer reasons for choosing you. This means *being different in ways that customers value*. As shown in Figure 12.1, there are four broad paths to being different:

1. Becoming the low-cost supplier.
2. Developing differentiated, innovative products and services.
3. Targeting a narrow niche (geography, industry, product/service).
4. Employing differentiated business methods and approaches.

Before we get to these, let's anchor our discussion to three premises.

Premise 1: Strategy Is a Process

That process begins with objective analysis of the external environment of customers, competitors, regulations, technologies, opportunities and threats, pricing constraints, and other factors. The process then turns inward, asking "What are our unique strengths and weaknesses? What unique capabilities do we bring to the market?" Strategy is formulated from that external and internal analysis. But it doesn't end there.

Strategy is not something that you can put in place at one moment and then neglect. The world of business is moving too fast for that. Today's winning strategy may be tomorrow's loser because of changes in the external environment. As you look back at Figure 5.1, you can imagine the impact of these turbulent changes on your business. And the greatest change is the global nature of present and future competition.

Figure 12.1 From Strategy to Superior Sustainable Performance

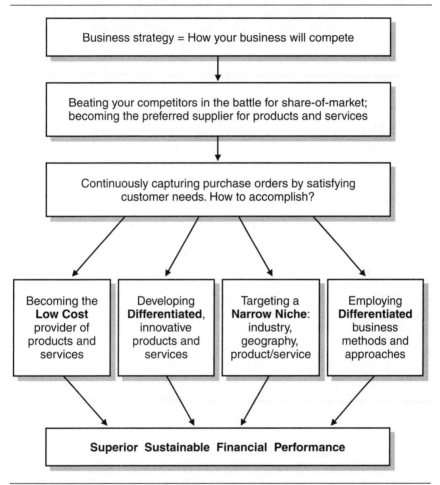

Source: www.CompetitiveSuccess.com, "From Strategy to Superior Sustainable Performance." Copyright © 2000 by Michael E. Gordon. Used with permission.

Premise 2: Your Products and Services Must Fill Real, and Urgent, Customer Wants and Needs

Boston-based ZipCar did that when it developed its member-based automobile company. Boston and other big cities are filled with people who walk to work or use public transportation. They don't own cars because cars are expensive and they have nowhere to park them. But every so often—perhaps once a week—these people need a car for a jaunt to the outlet mall, or to haul a load of Costco purchases, or for a week's vacation on the Maine coast. ZipCar fills that need by allowing members—for a fee—to use a car when they want for as long as they want. Car ownership is the traditional alternative to filling the driving needs of these customers, but ZipCar fills it better for many.

What customer need do you plan to satisfy with your product or service? For your target customers, can you serve that need better than other vendors? Failing to answer those questions correctly can be costly. The Polaroid Corporation, for example, lost $500 million in the development of instant movies. Polaroid's invention, PolaVision, was a technological marvel, but customers did not want it. The videocassette recorder preempted Polaroid's invention and gained rapid market acceptance.

Premise 3: Your Product or Service Must Work, Unambiguously

If it is flawed in any way and does not result in continuous customer satisfaction, your brilliant strategy will fail miserably. Worse, your competitors will have an opportunity to correct your mistakes and use your own strategy against you. As an example, our static control company developed an antistatic floor finish for use in microelectronic manufacturing facilities. It was an excellent concept. It provided a sorely needed solution to the problem of static generation on floor surfaces. Best of all, it was a consumable product, which meant that repeat orders would continue flowing in. Unfortunately, our product was not quite right technically; it was just marginally able to do the job. One of our competitors jumped on our weak product, improved it, and gained market dominance. We had to redevelop our product, urgently, to get back into the game— *in second position.*

FOUR BASIC APPROACHES TO GAINING COMPETITIVE ADVANTAGES

So strategy is about how your company will compete. At bottom, there are very few business strategies, though variations on these are limitless. Let's consider the four basic approaches. You can think up your own variations.

Becoming the Low-Cost Supplier

My family enjoys going to the outdoor Hay Market near the North End in downtown Boston to shop for fruits, vegetables, meat, and fish. It is a microcosm where customers come together with many suppliers having nondifferentiated products. Everyone can know the selling price for these virtually identical products: a pineapple is a pineapple, a cabbage is a cabbage, and my assumption is that the product *costs* to all of the competitors are about the same.

One approach to competing is to provide products or services at the lowest price, not merely by squeezing your own profits, but by creating a highly efficient operational system that wrings out costs. But Hay Market vendors do not have a cost advantage. So how do these vendors of commodity products gain competitive advantage? They don't! They compete aggressively on price alone, and this is the weakest of all strategies. The vendors all know the price point of maximum self-inflicted pain, below which they will not accept a sale. If your products and services are the same as your competitors', and the costs to you are the same, you also will tend to compete on price. This is a losing nonstrategy, unless you have an overarching strategic objective to capture market share first (dumping below cost, for example), becoming dominant, and then allowing prices to rise.

Wal-Mart

Wal-Mart has managed to dominate the retail business; customers will drive by other discount stores to shop there. Wal-Mart doesn't sell anything you cannot find elsewhere. Its parking lots are no more inviting than asphalt acres found elsewhere. Its store ambiance is strictly low-ball utilitarian. So why do people shop there? Because they can buy more goods for less money. Period.

To succeed with this low-price strategy, it takes more than a willingness to charge less than competitors. That tactic alone would result in a profitless race to the bottom. No, you must be able to charge less *and still make a good profit!* Wal-Mart has done this by wringing, squeezing, and extracting costs out of its global supply chain and retailing operations. It is the world's champion at this.

Adopt this strategy only if you can charge less than competitors *and* still have a decent profit margin.

Developing Differentiated, Innovative Products and Services

Providing unique and valuable product/service features and benefits that customers value is another proven strategy. And it is a powerful strategy for entering an established market in which the major competitors are clones of each other. This strategy is based on innovation. Consider the following examples:

Technological Innovation

In many cases, differentiation is achieved by means of a new technology. Toyota, for example, differentiated its Prius model by means of its hybrid gasoline-electric power source, one of the few truly significant innovations to come along since the auto industry adopted the internal combustion engine as its standard. That difference has been a winning ticket for the Prius. As of this writing, the company cannot keep up with demand.

Product Design Innovation

Product design can also be the differentiator. Sticking with the auto industry, consider the sturdy Volvo. Long before it became popular to do so, Volvo began designing its vehicles to protect drivers and passengers in a crash. Just as important, the company built its advertising messages around this point of differentiation, positioning its product as the safest car on the road. So, today, when most people think of passenger safety— for themselves and their family—they think Volvo.

Product Size Innovation

In response to the high price of fuel, DaimlerChrysler AG is introducing a two-seat minicar in the United States. Just 8.2 feet long, its "SmartforTwo" car gets 40 miles per gallon! No new technology, just a fuel-efficient car based on smallness.

Operational Innovation

Operational innovation can differentiate your product. Dell became a hugely successful PC maker by offering something different from IBM, Packard Bell, Hewlett-Packard, and dozens of other manufacturers. It gave the buyer a chance to order a custom-configured machine over the phone or Internet. No stores. No picking from four or five different models. Dell offered a huge spectrum of choice to buyers.

Innovative differentiation can come from *anywhere*. But to succeed you must assure the following:

- The point of differentiation must be real and verifiable.
- Customers must value the difference.
- The difference must be supported and reinforced through marketing messages.

Targeting a Niche: Geography, Industry, Product/Service

Targeting untapped or underserved geographic, industry, or product/service niches is a workable strategy. You may not be able to gain broad industry competitive advantages by going head-on, but you may be able to find a viable, focused opportunity in a particular market segment.

NetJets

NetJets, Inc.,[4] will never be a major air carrier, but it is successful in serving a small higher-end niche of the market. New Jersey-based NetJets offers fractional jet aircraft ownership to customers whose time is very valuable. For a one-eighth share, a typical customer may pay about $50,000 per year for customized jet transportation—no maintenance, no hassles. It is worth noting that the fractional ownership revenue model is another point of differentiation and innovation. At present, NetJets owns over 50 percent of this niche market.

Seabait Ltd.

Peter Cowin and Peter Olive, two entrepreneurs from the United Kingdom, filled an underserved market niche. They established their company, Seabait, Ltd., to farm sandworms for use as bait for sea fishermen. Using the heated effluent from a local power station, they are able to grow millions of sea worms year-round at very low costs. Their competitors were raking the ocean floor for these worms, as had been done for generations. Cowin and Olive's operational approach was so disruptive and cost-efficient that their competitors were thrown off balance. They realized they would not be able to compete unless they switched rapidly to worm farming. In the meantime, Seabait has extended its dominance by using these sandworms as a nutritious feed stock for the aquaculture of shrimp and fish. (For more information: www.seabait.com.) Note that Seabait developed three points of competitive advantage, leading to sustainability and profitability:

1. Tapping an underserved market niche.
2. Innovating the operational production of sandworms.
3. Expanding into other industries: aquaculture feedstock.

Employing Differentiated Business Methods and Approaches

In addition to (1) being the low-cost provider, (2) innovatively differentiating your product or service, and (3) focusing on a narrow niche, there is a fourth broad category for gaining competitive advantages: (4) business methods and approaches. This approach is limited only by your imagination. Here are the most common:

- Offering superior customer service (American Express, Marriott, IBM)
- Nurturing an entrepreneurial company culture (3M)
- Building unique core capabilities (Toyota)
- Commercializing proprietary know-how (Sony)
- Erecting barriers to competitor entry (Hewlett-Packard)
- Having unique access to markets (CVS)
- Moving quickly to gain first-mover advantage (UPS)
- Running faster, trying harder (Avis)
- Using your unbridled imagination

Note that all of these paths to competitive advantages are subsumed under the CUSTOMER model: Culture, Uniqueness, Strategy, Technology, Opportunity, Management, Execution, Resources, and the customer himself.

Many, many examples of business methods and approaches to gaining competitive advantages could be cited. With limited space, I will cite only one. However, I believe this to be the most important one: developing customer relationships and offering superior customer service.

Building strong customer relationships is an ideal way to differentiate your company from competitors. All other things being equal (similar costs, products, and services), wouldn't you rather deal with a company that treats you with great respect, like royalty, like a true friend? Many of the most successful companies have focused on customer relationships as a competitive advantage. Here are a few examples of taglines from some of the best:[5]

- *American Express:* "Heroic customer service"
- *IBM:* "Spend a lot of time making customers happy"

- *Marriott:* "Friendly service and excellent value" and "Customers are guests"
- *Nordstrom:* "Service to the customer above all else"

Absorb their best practices.

Customer Service

Excellent customer service will differentiate your products or services from those of your competitors. Even if yours is a commodity product or service—one that is identical to those of competitors—it may be possible to win customers through a strategy of service differentiation. For example, a friend of mine raves about his plumber. The Yellow Pages is full of plumbers, who all do basically the same thing. But my friend's plumber is different. When he shows up at the house, he and his assistant are clean-cut and nicely dressed. He cordially introduces his assistant and asks how the rest of the family is doing. When he leaves, the house is cleaner than when he arrived. This is a commodity service delivered with a difference that my friend values—and for which he pays extra.

Face to Face

In many respects, what goes on in today's commercial world can be categorized as either transactions or relationships. For example, I can now handle most of my personal financial needs without ever speaking to another human being. Thanks to the Internet and the phone system, I can buy and sell stock, obtain an extension on my bank line of credit, seek out and get an auto loan at the lowest rate, and purchase a bank CD for my IRA. Each of these transactions is low-cost and efficient.

On the other hand, I can do all of these things and more at my local bank, where a person I've known for a number of years listens to me, understands how my personal and business finances relate to each other, and occasionally suggests alternatives to my current approach to handling them. My banker is also a source of useful information about potential suppliers and others who might be able to help me: patent attorneys, tax specialists, and so forth. I value this type of relationship banking and so do millions of other people, even though it takes more time and costs a bit extra.

Though the trend appears to favor cheap, faceless, but efficient transactions, many customers prefer to buy from suppliers who work hard to understand and satisfy their needs.

A customer relationship strategy is feasible for many types of businesses and in many industries. Those that execute it well stand a good chance of gaining repeat business and a large share of wallet from each customer. If you adopt this strategy, however, you must assure that:

- Customers perceive a *tangible benefit* from their relationship with your company.
- Your products and services are flawless.
- Customers come away from every encounter feeling that they got more than they anticipated.

Although I've presented these basic strategy types as separate approaches, your goal is to strive for multiple points of competitive advantage by enabling as many approaches as possible. Exhibit 12.1 on pages 126 and 127 is a downloadable form to assist in implementation of your competitive strategy.

IMPLEMENTING YOUR STRATEGIC PLAN

Strategy is a never-ending, five-step process, from Opportunity to Customer Satisfaction:

Step 1: Formulate your statement of strategy.

Step 2: Identify, find, and communicate with potential customers.

Step 3: Exploit all ways to gain competitive advantages by differentiating, innovating, and adding unique value for your customers.

Step 4: Close the sale by becoming a world-class selling organization.

Step 5: Implement your customer relationship strategy with unsurpassed customer service.

You can visualize this five-step process by building onto the Money Machine as shown in Figure 12.2.

Step 1: Formulate Your Statement of Strategy

This statement need not be complex, but it does need to be astute. It will set the stage for how your company will compete. By way of example, the statement of strategy for our static control company follows:

Figure 12.2   The Strategic Money Machine

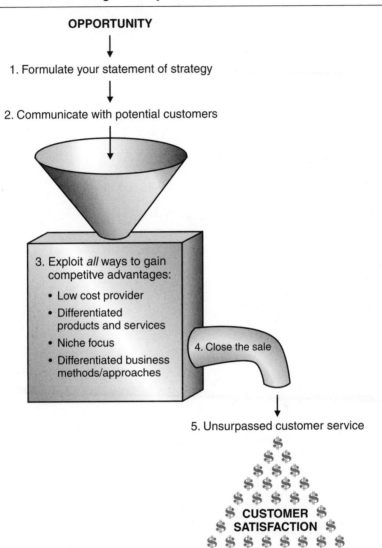

OPPORTUNITY

1. Formulate your statement of strategy

2. Communicate with potential customers

3. Exploit *all* ways to gain competitve advantages:
  - Low cost provider
  - Differentiated products and services
  - Niche focus
  - Differentiated business methods/approaches

4. Close the sale

5. Unsurpassed customer service

CUSTOMER SATISFACTION

Our company will compete in the emerging global static control industry using a three-pronged approach:

1. Aggressively and continuously developing innovative consumable products.
2. Relentlessly marketing and selling to the microelectronics industry through direct salespeople, sales representatives, international trade shows and global distributors.
3. Living the "heroic customer service" tagline of American Express by providing training and incentives to our customer-facing people.

Step 2: Identify, Find, and Communicate with All Potential Customers

This is the domain of marketing[6] and advertising. I have met many entrepreneurs who felt proud that they did little or no marketing, that they got new customers only by word of mouth. I am greatly disturbed by the concept of word-of-mouth advertising as a market penetration strategy. Yes, do create products and services that your customers appreciate—so much so that they will buzz and spread the word. But go out and proactively identify, find, and communicate with all potential customers. Hook them. Reel them in.

To do this, you must learn everything you can about all of your potential customers in your geographic market. Use the same sleuthing techniques you learned in Chapters 8 and 18 to ferret out information. Here are some leading questions:

- Specifically, who are your target customers?
- Do they cross several industries?
- If you are a business-to-business enterprise, what size company is the ideal target customer: small to medium, large, Fortune 500?
- Where are they located: in your immediate region, nationally, contiguous countries, broad global markets?
- Who specifically are you targeting inside the company?
- What are his or her buying criteria?
- How reachable are your customers?
- What resources do you have to locate all of your targeted customers?
- Are there must-go-to trade shows for your industry?
- Are there creative ways to penetrate global markets?
- What is the best way to reach them: print advertising, TV, radio, Internet, trade shows, direct mail?

This is only a starter list. The key is to find, identify, and communicate with *all* potential customers.

Step 3: Exploit All Ways to Gain Competitive Advantages by Differentiating, Innovating, and Adding Unique Value for Your Customers

Look inside your own Money Machine (Figure 12.2) to determine how you will gain competitive advantages. To add differentiated, significant value, you must understand your customers' needs and how your product or service will be used by the customer. Michael Porter's Value Chain[7] is a tool for exploring points of entry into your customer's realm. The Value Chain breaks down your *buyer's activities* into separate, understandable pieces. And this presents possibilities of finding ways to add unique customer value. Here are some questions to consider:

- Do you understand specifically how your customer is using your product?
- Can you devise many other ways that your product could be more valuable to your customer: special packaging, unique dimensions, innovative technology, different materials, tailored services, others?
- What bells and whistles are important to your customer?
- What skills, experiences, and core capabilities does your company have to add customer value?
- What else will the customer value in your relationship?

Remember to look inside the money machines of your competitors, as well. Borrow their best practices, and then go beyond. Innovate!

Step 4: Close the Sale

This is where strategy crosses the finish line. Picture this: You have implemented an exceptional strategy and (1) differentiated your product or service from the competition, (2) created significant perceived customer value, and (3) found, identified, and communicated with potential customers. Your strategy is working. Many potential customers are now pouring into the top of your Money Machine. But this is not the end of the strategy story. You must do something to get them through the machine and to the cash register at the other end—closing the deal. In most cases, that happens through effective selling.

Some sales systems and some salespeople are more successful than others. Consider John Essler and Joe Girard. In 1997, John Essler[8] purchased three exclusive dealership agreements from Craft-Bilt Manufacturing Company, a company that made prebuilt sunrooms. Essler studied the top, the middle, and the bottom of his own sales funnel to generate leads and to close customers. After all, this was one of his main keys to success. For every 100 leads, 37 would actually set up appointments, but only 10 sales would result, that is, a 10 percent closing rate. His funnel looked like this:

Advertising $$ > 100 names > 37 appointments > 10 sales

But Essler wanted a greater percentage of closures. He set up a sales system based on (1) targeted advertising, (2) demonstrating completed sunrooms, (3) attractive sales incentives for his sales personnel, and (4) thorough training of sales personnel. He succeeded, and his closing rate increased dramatically!

Joe Girard has a similar story, which he shares in his book *How to Sell Anything to Anybody.*[9] In the introduction, he declared himself to be the world's greatest salesman, pointing to the *Guinness Book of World Records* to verify his claim.

Girard was selling commodity products: Chevrolet cars and trucks that could be sold by thousands of other salespeople. Girard's noteworthy success was the creation of a powerful sales system that built long-term relationships, referrals, incentives, and customer satisfaction. He realized that he had no competitive advantages based on product or cost. However, his dogged persistence ensured that more leads went into the top of his sales funnel, and his customer-centric manner led to a greater percentages of closings. That's how Joe became the world's greatest salesman! His book is worth reading.

Step 5: Implement Your Customer Relationship Strategy with Unsurpassed Customer Service

Building strong customer relationships requires an action plan that, at a minimum, includes the following:

- Well-trained customer-facing employees with good people skills
- Incentives that reward employees for building strong and profitable customer relationships
- An information system that keeps track of customers, their needs, and their current transactions with you

- A company culture that puts customers on a pedestal
- A system for measuring how well your company is performing its relationship role *as perceived by customers*

Having a strategy will put you in the game, but you need more to win. Specifically, you need to execute your strategy very well. Regrettably, many entrepreneurs—as well as corporate executives—fail to execute well. Poor execution usually results in business *"execution."*

Though a full discussion of implementation is beyond the scope of this primer, the importance of solid implementation cannot be overstated. In fact, a so-so strategy flawlessly implemented is more powerful than a great strategy implemented indifferently. Aim for the *best strategy and the best implementation.*

SUMMARY

Entrepreneurial strategy is the process of gaining competitive advantages for the purpose of earning robust, sustainable profits by satisfying customer needs. In plain language, that means winning profitable purchase orders and continuously beating your competitors in the battle for share of market. Five approaches to gaining competitive advantages were discussed:

1. Becoming the low-cost provider of products and services.
2. Developing differentiated, innovative products and services.
3. Targeting a narrow niche: geography, industry, product/service.
4. Employing differentiated business methods and approaches.
5. Exploiting all nine factors of Gordon's CUSTOMER Model.

A five-step framework was presented to implement your strategic battle plan.

Actions

√ Reread and apply the messages from this chapter to your business. There is sustaining "meat" here.

√ Uncover your competitors' strategies. Incorporate the best components into your own strategic plan. Innovate beyond them.

√ Develop a quantitative, measurable plan for implementing each of the five strategic steps.

√ Keep one eye on your customer, one eye on each of your competitors, and one eye on your company's core competencies. That's a lot of eyes.

Downloadable Exhibit 12.1   Sources of Competitive Advantage*

	Competitive Advantages	Implementation	Your Actions
1	Become the low-cost provider of products and services	Establish a system that can produce or deliver products and services at lowest possible cost.	
2	Develop differentiated, innovative products and services	Provide unique product/service features that are not readily available from other suppliers.	
3	Target a narrow niche: geography, industry, product/service	Gain competitive advantage by finding a geographic niche, an underserved or untapped market niche, or a product/service niche.	
4–12	Employ a variety of differentiated business methods and approaches		
4	Create a unique brand	Consider the competitive advantages of these world-class brands: Trump, Coke, iPod, Harley-Davidson, M&M's.	
5	Offer superior customer service; developing strong customer relationships	Customers prefer to buy from suppliers who work hard to satisfy their needs. This should be the pillar of every company.	
6	Nurture an entrepreneurial company culture	Unleash the power of an internal culture based on innovation and customer focus.	
7	Build unique core capabilities	Differentiate capabilities that give your company advantages.	

Exhibit 12.1   Continued

	Competitive Advantages	Implementation	Your Actions
8	Commercialize proprietary know-how	Develop proprietary processes or formulations, patents, licensed technology.	
9	Erect barriers to future competitor entry	Create a customer-preferred brand, patent, or geographic dominance.	
10	Act decisively to capture first-mover advantage	Exploit unique innovations with urgency; enter an emerging market; ride the wave.	
11	Gain unique access to markets and channels of distribution	Penetrate channels of distribution; employ unique sales/marketing methods.	
12	Run faster, try harder	The world of commerce is moving at hyperspeed.	
13–21	Gordon's CUSTOMER Model for competitive advantages	Commit to Culture, Uniqueness, Strategy, Technology, Opportunity, Management, Execution, and Resources to gain competitive advantages.	

13

PROJECT YOUR GROWTH
AND PROFITABILITY

Money (also referred to as cash or capital) is literally the fluid of life for your business. If ever your Money Machine is drained of this vital fluid, the game is over. This is not something you can leave to chance. You *must* gain a working knowledge of financial statements[1] and understand what they tell you about the well-being of your business. If you are not familiar with financial statements, do not be concerned. They will be demystified as we go through them step by step. In this chapter, you learn about four quantitative tools you can use to understand your business:

1. The cash flow statement tells you how much cash moves into and out of your business over a particular time period, and how much cash remains. It also defines where the cash came from and where it went.
2. The balance sheet answers the question: What are my assets, liabilities, and net worth of my business at any moment of time?
3. The income statement (also known as statement of profit and loss) measures the profitability of your business over a stated period.
4. Breakeven analysis will tell you what level of sales will cover your expenses.

CASH FLOW AND GRANDMA

My grandmother Anna understood cash flow very clearly. Her husband, Saul, earned a meager living as a cobbler in Lithuania during the time of the Russian Revolution. Mustering all of their courage, Saul and Anna fled from Lithuania in hopes of a better life in America. They literally had nothing but a few hundred dollars (sewn into his cuffs) and the clothes they wore on the ship. Saul decided that he would continue to make his livelihood as a cobbler in the United States because shoe repair was the only business he knew. Borrowing money from a few acquaintances, he set up a small work area inside a friend's tailor shop and began to build his business. So, how did Anna come to understand cash flow, when many MBA students have trouble with this concept? Simple: her cigar box! Money from any and all sources from and for Saul's shoe repair business went into the cigar box; all of the expenditures came out of the cigar box. Anna watched that cigar box like a hawk. Figure 13.1 shows the simplicity of cash flow.

At the end of each day, week, month, and year Anna would count the remaining money in the cigar box. Because she collected all the money and paid all the bills, she always knew precisely what was coming in, what was going out, and what was left in the cigar box. In those months when more went out than came in, she understood the consequences of negative cash flow on a real *gut* level. "Saul, can't you repair more shoes? How about repairing leather coats?"

There are many ways that cash can come into and go out of your business, as shown in Exhibit 13.1. The important point to note is that your cigar box only accounts for money that was actually received and spent. It does not account for money owed to you or for bills yet to be paid. Cash flow is the single most important financial tool to let you know the amount of life fluid there is in your company at any one moment in time.

Figure 13.1 Grandma's Cigar Box

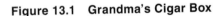
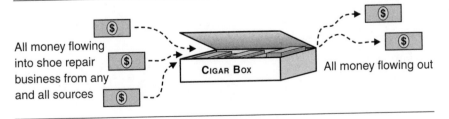

All money flowing into shoe repair business from any and all sources

CIGAR BOX

All money flowing out

Downloadable Exhibit 13.1   Cash Flow Analysis of Saul's Business*

	January ($)	February ($)	etc.
Beginning of monthly cash balance	0	160	
Cash Inflows			
Cash actually received from customers for sale of products or services	80	95	
Cash received from sale of assets	0	0	
Cash received from loans	100	0	
Cash received from other financing: personal savings; money received from family, friends, other investors	100	0	
Cash received from interest on investments	0	0	
Cash received from sale of stock	0	0	
Cash received from all other sources	0	0	
Total cash inflows	280	95	
Cash Outflows			
Payments for all operating expenses (rent, salaries, insurance, marketing materials, supplies, electricity, etc.)	20	40	
Payments for actual purchases of inventory	50	30	
Payments for taxes	0	0	
Payments for acquisition of assets (table, anvil, tools)	50	0	
Repayment of loans (including interest and principle)	0	10	
Payments for bonuses, life insurance, auto	0	0	

Exhibit 13.1 Continued

	January ($)	February ($)	etc.
Payments for legal and accounting services	0	0	
Payments for all other items	0	0	
Total cash outflows	120	80	
Cash Inflows Minus Outflows	160	15	
Ending Cash Balance (cash remaining in the cigar box)	160 (Goes on top of next column)	175 (Goes on top of next column)	

Source: www.CompetitiveSuccess.com, "Cash Flow Analysis of Saul's Business." Copyright © 2000 by Michael E. Gordon. Used with permission. *A blank version of this page can be downloaded from www.trumpuniversity.com/entrepreneurship101 for your personal use.*

THE BALANCE SHEET AND GRANDFATHER'S BANKER

My grandfather's business grew. In addition to shoe repair, he began to offer other services (leather coat refurbishing, leather handbag repair) and some products (belts, polishes, shoelaces). He rented a little more space and hired an assistant. Cash flow was becoming problematic because of the need for working capital for salaries, inventory, rent, and all other business expenses. Saul set up a meeting with a banker, and the second thing the banker said to Saul was "Let's have a look at your financials, and particularly, your balance sheet." He went on to explain to Saul what a balance sheet is and why it is so important to the bank. He pointed out that banks lend money only against business and personal assets as collateral against default on the loan. Banks also look closely at the income and cash flow statements because they need to understand the borrower's ability to repay loans faithfully from cash flow. Banks do not want to own the assets: inventory, real estate, equipment, or any other nonliquid assets pledged as collateral. In the unpleasant circumstance that Saul could not repay the loan, the bank would need to sell the collateral assets. Saul was getting an education on the importance of the balance sheet and the other two financial statements.

The balance sheet is a snapshot showing the financial condition of your company at a particular moment in time, usually at year's end. The formula for the balance sheet is simple:

$$\text{Net worth of your business} = \text{Assets} - \text{Liabilities}$$

Assets are everything that is owned by your business, and that is owed to your business.

Liabilities are everything that your business owes, including debts and claims that creditors have against the assets of your company.

Net worth is what the business is worth after all liabilities have been satisfied.

Exhibit 13.2 is a typical balance sheet format.

The balance sheet can be thought of as a summary report on the results of a medical examination of your business. Is your business healthy or unhealthy? The healthiest businesses have robust assets and net worth and minimal liabilities. The weakest businesses are just the opposite: skimpy assets and net worth and life-threatening liabilities. As a rule of thumb, the ratio of total current assets to total current liabilities (known as the *current ratio*) is used by lenders as an indicator of a company's ability to repay loans. For safety, the current ratio should be greater than 2. Another widely used measure of the company's relative debt burden is the ratio of total liabilities to net worth (known as *debt to equity ratio*). This ratio should stay well below 1.

THE INCOME STATEMENT

This financial statement lets you know, or predict, how much money you are making from the actual *operation* of your business. It provides a straightforward tool for measuring whether your company is profitable or unprofitable by comparing all revenue streams to all expenses.

Let's assume you have been in business for one month and have begun to generate sales. Here is how you would prepare a simplified income statement for the first month of operation of your business (Exhibit 13.3):

Step 1: Add up all of your sales revenue for the first month.

Step 2: Subtract your costs to produce the product or to deliver the service. This is called cost of goods sold, or COGS.

Downloadable Exhibit 13.2   Balance Sheet*

	Today ($)	One Year (Projected $)
Current Assets		
Cash		
Accounts receivable		
Inventory and supplies		
Short-term investments		
Prepaid expenses		
Other current assets		
Total current assets		
Fixed Assets		
Land and buildings		
Building improvements		
Furniture		
Equipment/Machinery		
Autos/Vehicles		
Other assets		
Long-term investments		
Total Current + Fixed Assets		
Current Liabilities		
Accounts payable		
Notes payable		
Deferred income taxes		
Payroll owed		
Total current liabilities		
Long-Term Liabilities		
Long-term debt		
Long-term contractual commitments		
Total liabilities		
Net Worth = Assets – Liabilities (Net worth, also referred to as equity or book value, includes all earnings retained in the company plus all capital that has been invested in exchange for ownership of the company.)		

Step 3: This equals your gross profits (gross profit margin).

Step 4: Subtract all other operating costs not related to COGS.

Step 5: This is your operating profit (also called profit from operations [PFO] or earnings before interest, taxes, depreciation, amortization[EBITDA]).

There is nothing challenging here except for the costs, and there are only two categories of costs to understand: cost of goods sold and operating costs.

Cost of Goods Sold

This is the cost to produce or purchase your product (including materials, inventory change during the month, labor, packaging, commissions, freight into your company) or to perform your service (hourly rate, supplies, expenses for travel to client, entertainment, miscellaneous service-related costs).

Operating Costs

These costs remain constant; they do not vary with your sales volume. These are the costs of keeping your doors open, whether or not any product is produced or service delivered. Operating costs include rent, insurance, administrative salaries, telephone, utilities, legal and accounting services, marketing, advertising, auto, travel, Internet connection, supplies, repairs, maintenance, postage, research and development, and all costs not directly related to the actual production of products or delivery of services.

Let's look at a simplified format for the income statement (Exhibit 13.3).

I have called it the simplified income statement. If you are not familiar with these financial statements, they certainly do not appear to be simple. Had your accountant produced it, the format would show greater detail. For example, profit from operations would be refined further to account for interest, taxes, depreciation, and amortization. For now, you do not need these refinements to understand the operation of your business.

Assumptions

Your income statement is built on certain *assumptions* that you make regarding income and costs, and these assumptions provide the numbers for

Downloadable Exhibit 13.3   Simplified Income Statement*

	Description	Calculation	Month 1 ($)	% of Total Revenue (TR)
	Sales revenue from Product A	Income (or sales) from Product A		
	Sales revenue from Product B	Income (or sales) from Product B		
	Sales revenue from Service C	Income (or sales) from Service C		
1	Total revenues from income streams A, B, and C (TR)	Total amount of sales A + B + C		100%
2	Cost of goods sold (COGS): All product costs—materials, inventory change during the month, freight into your company, commissions, packaging, and labor to produce your product. All costs to perform your services—hourly rate, supplies, expenses for travel to client, entertainment, and miscellaneous service-related costs.	All costs to produce your product or to deliver your services. Figure out product and service costs carefully.		COGS x 100 ÷ by TR
3	Gross profit margin (GPM)	Row 1 – Row 2		GPM x 100 ÷ by TR
4	Total operating costs (TOC): Rent, insurance, nonproduction salaries, telephone, utilities, legal and accounting services, marketing, advertising, auto, travel, Internet connection, supplies, repairs, maintenance, postage, and all other operating expenses.	If not one dollar of sales occurred, the business would still have these expenses just to keep the doors open.		TOC x 100 ÷ by TR
5	Profit (or loss) from Operations (PFO): also known as Earnings before interest, taxes, depreciation, amortization (EBITDA).	Row 3 – Row 4 THIS IS THE IMPORTANT NUMBER!		PFO x 100 ÷ by TR

your income statement. The key is to define your assumptions carefully; good things will then follow. To illustrate, let's look at two types of businesses. The first is a product business, Bookstore Café; the other is a service business, On-Site Computer Training Company. What income and cost assumptions can we make for each of these businesses? These assumptions are shown in Exhibit 13.4.

Total Operating Costs

Revenues, cost of goods sold and gross profit margin are only one side of the equation. However, if not one dollar of sales occurred, the business would still have operating costs. Your task is to develop this list of operating costs for your own business using Exhibit 13.5 as a template. To help you zero in, consider a range of values for each line item, optimistic, pessimistic, and most likely. Fill in your values and arrive at an amount for total operating costs (TOC).

It is now time to apply what you are learning to your own business. Refer back to Exhibit 13.3 on page 135 and slowly crawl through each row with me. For now, fill in your numbers for one month only. Estimate numbers for the first month that you *predict* sales. If you already have sales, use the last full month's numbers:

Row 1: Total revenues (TR) ($). How many streams of revenue do you predict for Month 1? Account for each separately, then add them together to arrive at TR for Month 1. To be more thorough, you could predict a range for each revenue stream, spanning the spread from optimistic, to pessimistic, to most likely. Your first cut at projections for the income statement would use the "most likely" value.

Row 2: Cost of goods sold (COGS) ($). Now you need to factor in what it costs you to produce your products or to perform your services. The costs for a product company are the sum of labor, materials, packaging, commissions, and freight into your company. This is the COGS. Using the example of Bookstore Café, the average customer would pay $20 for a book that costs you $10 from a distributor. However, the book must be shipped to your store, and then there is a bit of labor involved in receiving it and putting it on the shelf. If we assume that the actual cost of the book to you as it sits on the shelf is $12, that is the COGS.

For a service business, as in the example of On-Site Computer Training, let's assume that you are performing four hours of

Downloadable Exhibit 13.4   Assumptions*

Type of Business	Bookstore Café	On-Site Computer Training
	Products	Services
How do you make money? Where do revenues (also called sales) come from?	You have two income streams: - Sale of books, plus - Food products	Your revenue stream comes from your hourly billing rate multiplied by the number of hours of training your client.
What is the price your customer pays for product or service? Note the distinction between the price the customer pays you and the cost to you for each book.	Assumptions: The average price the customer pays per book is $20. On average, each customer buys one book and $1 of food from the cafe.	Assumptions: Your client pays $50 for each training hour, which includes your travel time. The average client hires you for 4 hours, for a total of $200.
What is your cost to provide these products or services? This is the cost of goods sold (COGS).	Assumptions: The average cost you pay per book is $10. You also have to pay shipping costs to get it to your company, plus labor to put it on the shelf. Assume $2 per book. $12 (book COGS) + $0.50 (food COGS) = $12.50 / book buyer.	Assumptions: Your costs to deliver this consulting service include hourly rate, expenses for travel to client, office supplies, and entertainment, amounting to $50 per client if you perform the service. If your employee performs the service, the COGS to your company would include his or her hourly rate.
Number of products or services sold per month or year	Assumptions: Your store will be open 365 days per year. You anticipate that you will sell 1,500 books per month and 18,000 books per year.	Assumptions: You anticipate that you will have 50 clients per month, 600 clients per year, each paying $200 on average.
Total sales revenue per month	Books: 1,500 x $20 Food: 1,500 x $1 Total: $31,500	Monthly consulting sales: 50 x $200 Total: $10,000

(continued)

Exhibit 13.4   Continued

Type of Business	Bookstore Café	On-Site Computer Training
Gross profit per month (revenue – COGS)	$12,750 ($31,500 – $18,750)	$7,500 ($10,000 – $2500)
Total revenue per year	$378,000	$120,000
Gross profit margin per year (revenue – COGS)	$153,000 ($378,000 – $225,000)	$90,000 ($120,000 – $30,000)
Total operating costs (TOC)	<u>Assumptions:</u> $90,000	<u>Assumptions:</u> $24,000
Profit from Operations (known as EBITDA)	$63,000 ($153,000 – $90,000)	$66,000 ($90,000 – $24,000)

Source: www.CompetitiveSuccess.com, "Assumptions." Copyright © 2000 by Michael E. Gordon. Used with permission. *A blank version of this page can be downloaded from www.trumpuniversity.com/entrepreneurship101 for your personal use.*

consultation, for which your client pays $50 per hour ($200 total). Your COGS might include automobile expenses, other transportation, office supplies, lunch, and miscellaneous expenses, amounting to $50. If an employee of yours performs the service, his or her hourly cost must also be included.

Row 2: COGS (percent). It is very enlightening to express COGS (and all other numbers as well) as a percentage of TR, which would be COGS ($) multiplied by 100 and divided by TR. This allows you to compare percentages from period to period. Are you doing better or worse, not from the absolute numbers, but from the percentages?

Row 3: Gross profit margin (GPM) ($). Row 1 minus Row 2.

Row 3: GPM (percent). Equals GPM ($) multiplied by 100 and divided by TR.

Row 4: Total operating costs (TOC) ($). The total of all costs and expenses from Exhibit 13.5.

Row 4: TOC (percent). Equals TOC ($) multiplied by 100 and divided by TR.

Downloadable Exhibit 13.5   Total Operating Costs*

Expenses	Optimistic ($)	Pessimistic ($)	Most Likely ($) (Use this column)
Rent			
Insurance			
Office salaries			
Telephone			
Heat			
Electricity			
Legal			
Accounting			
Supplies			
Internet access			
Repairs			
Maintenance			
Postage			
Marketing			
Advertising			
Auto			
Entertainment			
Travel			
Sales administration			
Research and development			
Other operating costs			
Total operating costs (TOC)			TOC (Use this number to calculate breakeven)

Row 5: PFO ($). Comes from subtracting Row 4 from Row 3.

Row 5: PFO (percent). Equals PFO ($) multiplied by 100 and divided by TR.

By way of summary, what do these numbers tell you? Total revenue tells you how much money is coming into your company from the sale of products and services. Cost of goods sold tells you how much it actually costs to produce or deliver these products and services. Gross profit margin tells you how much actual profit you make *before* subtracting operating costs. *Profit from Operations* (also known as EBITDA) is the most important row on your income statement. Plain and simple, it tells you how much money your Money Machine actually earns from *operations.* It is interesting to see the big picture emerging. Successful entrepreneurs are able to find the balance between keeping total operating costs and cost of goods sold to an effective minimum while maximizing sales revenue. *Do not accept a negative PFO!*

Are you wondering what the difference is between the income statement and the cash flow statement? The income statement measures whether your company is profitable or unprofitable by comparing all revenue streams to all expenses. At the end of the year, for example, not all money has actually been received or paid. Depending on the accounting method used, these are embedded in the income statement and the balance sheet. However, the cash flow statement will not include these items because they have not actually been paid or received. Also, money that you have borrowed from lenders or received from investors will not be accounted for in profit from operations because they do not relate to revenue streams or expenses from the actual operation of your business. They will, however, show up in the cash flow statement.

BREAKEVEN ANALYSIS

Breakeven analysis is a method for determining how much a company must sell to break even on a fixed investment. It is the exact point where sales cover all costs, as described in the following equation:

$$\text{Breakeven sales} = \text{Total operating costs} + \text{Cost of goods sold}$$

Breakeven is simple to calculate, yet crucial in its ability to yield a measurable target of profitability. As you are running your business, revenue will be flowing in due to your selling activities, and money will be flowing out to cover expenses. At what point has your business become profitable?

Once you hit the breakeven point, the next dollar of sales results in a profitable contribution to your company. At that point, it is time to pop the cork. You have succeeded! The next equation lets you define this point quantitatively:

$$\text{Breakeven sales} = \frac{\text{Total operating costs}}{\dfrac{\text{Gross profit margin}}{\text{Total revenues}}}$$

Let's assume that in the start-up of Bookstore Café (Exhibit 13.4), the annual total operating costs were \$90,000, the annual gross profit margin was \$153,000, and the total revenues were \$378,000:

$$\text{Annual breakeven sales} = \frac{\$90,000}{\left(\dfrac{\$153,000}{\$378,000}\right)} = \$225,000$$

When Bookstore Café reaches annual sales of \$225,000, it is at breakeven. To know what sales it needs on a monthly basis to reach breakeven, simply divide by 12:

$$\text{Monthly breakeven sales} = \frac{\$225,000}{12} = \$18,750$$

This is quite an important number, and the graph in Figure 13.2 permits you to visualize the precise monthly sales point at which your company has turned profitable. In this example, breakeven sales were reached between the eighth and ninth months. Remember that these projections are only as accurate as your *assumptions*.

You can see why breakeven analysis is so satisfying. It takes the mystery out of the precise point of profitability.

SUMMARY

In this chapter, we have studied the four essential financial statements you need to monitor, control, and predict the well-being of your Money

Machine: income, cash flow, breakeven sales, and balance sheet. There is no choice. You *must* gain a working knowledge of these financial statements. Otherwise, you run the risk of building a moneyless machine!

Actions

Make a commitment right now:

√ *You are really going to start your new venture as you read this book.*
√ You will reach zero-stage within four months from today (Chapter 6) and breakeven sales six months later.
√ Carefully develop your assumptions only for the first year for each statement, using today as the starting point.
√ Develop a draft projection of cash flow and income statements, monthly for the first 12 months of operation. Use the 13th column to aggregate all 12 months.
√ Develop your breakeven analysis to determine the month of profitability. Your breakeven sales projection should look like Figure 13.2.

Figure 13.2   Monthly Sales Compared to Breakeven Sales

Monthly Sales $	Jan.	Feb.	Mar.	Apr.	May	Jun.	Jul.	Aug.	Sep.	Oct.	Nov.	Dec.
50,000												
40,000												
35,000												
30,000												X	X
25,000						Breakeven sales				X		
20,000	Monthly operating costs								X			
15,000							X	X				
10,000					X	X						
5,000		X	X	X								
0	X											

Source: www.CompetitiveSuccess.com, "Monthly Sales Compared to Breakeven Sales." Copyright © 2000 by Michael E. Gordon. Used with permission.

Pep Talk

This is a challenge and a half. I used to view financial literacy as a difficult nuisance. It is so much easier to be an armchair philosopher, viewing the world from 20,000 feet. I learned the hard way. Businesses sink because of financial illiteracy. If you have little familiarity with these concepts, don't be daunted. Just take one small step at a time as you prepare each financial statement. *The journey of 1,000 miles begins with the first step.*

14

MOBILIZE POWERFUL

RESOURCES QUICKLY

One of the most complex public works projects in the history of the United States is targeted for completion in 2007 in downtown Boston. This massive construction project has four goals: to bury the overhead route of Interstate 93 under the city; to make land available for parks and people; to construct a second underwater tunnel to the airport; and to integrate the waterfront with the rest of the city. This is an *immense* undertaking, one that required the project's managers to marshal massive financial, physical, knowledge, infrastructure, and people resources (Figure 14.1). Whenever I pass any of the construction sites, I am reminded of how entrepreneurs must likewise marshal and manage productive resources to accomplish their goals.

Great accomplishments require powerful resources. Entrepreneurial resources are anything, absolutely anything, that can move your venture further and faster with least risk. Like the cranes in the photograph, each one contributes to the progress and eventual completion of the project. The loss of any one crane would slow the project down. In the extreme, the absence of all cranes would result in a small, slow-moving activity of very limited scope. The same will happen to your venture if you fail to harness adequate resources.

Figure 14.1   Construction Site in Downtown Boston

Source: "The Big Dig's Most Visible Workers Talk about Life on the Seat of the Project's Huge Cranes" by Nathan Cobb, *Boston Globe,* September 8, 1998. Photo by Tom Herde, *Boston Globe.* Reprinted with permission.

This chapter aims to shape your thinking on the power of entrepreneurial resources to start and grow your business. It identifies the types of resources you need and explains how to mobilize them.[1]

ENTREPRENEURIAL RESOURCES ARE DIFFERENT

By necessity, entrepreneurs think differently about resources. The dilemma is that they need a vast array of resources, yet they are habitually strapped for cash. Rather than lamenting their circumstances, successful entrepreneurs focus on *how to:* How can I mobilize the necessary resources with limited capital? They will not let the lack of money stop them or slow them down. As a basic approach to resource mobilization and management, successful entrepreneurs seek to:

- Bootstrap to conserve financial resources (Chapter 7)
- Do things themselves
- Negotiate and barter for everything they need (Chapter 16)

- Obtain free resources whenever possible
- Use other people's resources
- Control resources, rather than own them
- Borrow, rent, or lease
- Maintain flexibility so that they are not locked into physical resources that become anchors
- Use copious amounts of imagination and street smarts

No matter what size or type of company, mustering your needed resources can make the difference between success and nonsuccess.

Entrepreneurial resources fall into six categories: people, physical, financial, knowledge, infrastructure, and your imagination, as shown in Figure 14.2.

People Resources

People resources are the most important of all resources. This is self-evident: Take people out of the equation and there is no equation. Yet entrepreneurs often neglect the systematic building and nurturing of these

Figure 14.2   Six Categories of Entrepreneurial Resources

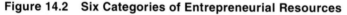

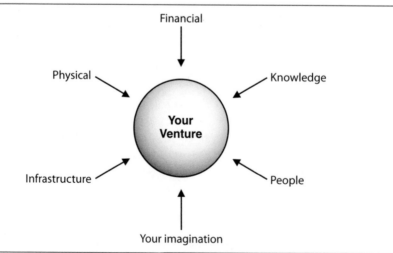

Source: www.CompetitiveSuccess.com, "Six Categories of Entrepreneurial Resources." Copyright © 2004 by Michael E. Gordon. Used with permission.

crucial resources. People resources include you, your partner(s), company culture, management team, business advisors, mentors, directors, door openers, business service professionals, family, friends, and all other stakeholders.

You

The ultimate resource for your venture is you. Entrepreneurs often neglect themselves in the intensity of their entrepreneurial voyage. Do pay particular attention to your own personal, emotional, and physical needs. In addition to spending quality time with family and friends, I made sure to allocate personal time for sports, reading, music, hiking, and quiet moments by myself. *Your burnout can result in your business flameout.*

Partners

I was fortunate to have been in business with a great partner and friend, Len Cohen. We worked together effectively and synergistically, accomplishing more together than either one of us could have achieved alone. We were constantly strategizing; solving problems; making decisions; taking action; worrying about competition, employees, and financial problems; laughing; traveling; going head-to-head over difficult issues; getting stuck, getting unstuck, and basking in our entrepreneurial accomplishments. We were great resources for our business and for each other. Not all partnerships are productive. Ours was.

Management Team

We developed a highly motivated, talented, justshowupandgetitdone management team. When we started our business, we merely sought to hire the best talent we could afford, one person at a time. Over the years, our managers increased their own individual skills and absorbed our work attitudes, integrity, customer-centricity, humor, enthusiasm, and goal orientation. They coalesced into a success-oriented team. To a very large extent, your management team will also absorb your characteristics, values, energy, and passions.

Company Culture

We built a success culture. As I began writing this section, I had a strong desire to travel back in time to reexperience our company culture. Fortunately, there remain a few videotapes of our Christmas parties. What I reexperienced was very exhilarating. There were two parts to the festivities. The first part was a year-end review of all significant business, financial, and strategic issues, including frank discussions of the company's strengths, weaknesses, opportunities, and threats. The second part was a side-splitting presentation of silly, very personalized gifts to many of our employees. The gifts were unique; they could not be purchased. Each one had to be cobbled together from bizarre materials. A story would accompany each weird gift. The laughter was nonstop.

I realize now how important this was. We were sending two messages to our people: First, they were a valued team of insiders that were privy to our confidential information; second, they were treated individually on a very personal basis. They were recognized. They were not just human machines. Watching the video made me proud of the familylike success culture we created.

Advisors

Something happened that almost sunk our company. Years earlier, we had hired a very bright young woman whose job grew as our business grew. Over the years, she took on marketing, operations, customer service, purchasing, the office function, and more. She was at the center of many of our activities. One day, she gave us notice that she would be leaving. *This was devastating news!* Without her, we wondered if our business would survive. After many exhaustive discussions with our advisors (valuable people resources), we decided not to hire her replacement. Rather, we would begin to hire a replacement for each of her functions—five people in all: managers of operations, sales, administration, marketing, and bookkeeping. Within one year, our organization became very strong, and every function was getting appropriate attention. Even our own job functions became crystal clear: My partner focused on developing new products and I devoted my attention to international marketing.

Building a strong management team was the turning point in the life of our company. Yet, Len and I would not have made the risky financial decision to build the organization so quickly. We were conservative by nature. Our professional advisors were invaluable in reshaping our thinking. We made it a point to surround ourselves with the best advisors, mentors, and door openers of all kinds—anyone and everyone that could help us make the best decisions.

Business Service Providers

A realtor called and asked me to meet her at an investment property in Boston within one hour. She wanted me to be the first to look at a three-story building with medical offices on the first floor and residential apartments above. I toured the building with her and was intrigued. We signed an Offer to Purchase that day, and I wrote a $1,000 check as a good faith deposit, to be held in escrow by the realtor.

The timing was very short. I had 10 days to make the decision to take the next step and sign the Purchase and Sale Agreement. Under pressure to make a rapid, but correct, decision, my first thought went to resources. I began to mobilize a network of knowledgeable business service providers: a commercial building inspector, an architect, a contractor, leasing agents, the city engineer, and my banker. I already had a great real estate lawyer, Bruce Miller, who was available to respond on short notice. Information had to be gathered from the city about acceptable uses for the building, as well as any restrictions. Also needed was an understanding of the rental market for medical offices and condos in this location. If everything looked good, substantial money had to be mobilized quickly.

So what did happen? The building was inspected within eight days, and my conclusion was not to proceed based on the inspection report. My $1,000 check was returned, and I paid the building inspector $250. In the interim period, I had tapped into a network of knowledgeable business service providers. And these professionals are now available to me for the next potential real estate deal.

Tip: Build and nurture a network of talented professionals, including bankers, real estate and business brokers, lawyers, accountants, contractors, and a board of advisors, who will be available when needed.

Family and Friends

Being an entrepreneur can be lonely, especially in the early stages. And the pressure to maintain momentum with limited resources can be hydraulic. Every bit of emotional support is a gift. I have been truly blessed in having my dear family members, friends, and colleagues in my life. They made and continue to make all the difference. Thank you all!

Physical Resources

A guiding principle in entrepreneurship is to *control*, rather than to own, physical resources. Real estate, equipment, machinery, manufacturing capabilities, and research facilities are physical resources, and very capital-intensive ones at that. By using physical resources that belong to other companies, you will reduce risk, enlist proprietary knowledge, and gain maximum flexibility. By way of example, we had an idea for a static-dissipative table and floor mat made from fiberglass materials. However, we had neither a development laboratory for this technology nor a manufacturing facility. We didn't even know how to formulate the product because it was in such a specific area of plastic materials. All we had was a concept, a recognition of customer need, and the ability to specify precisely what those customers needed—nothing else. I say nothing else, but I did have the ability to win-win negotiate (Chapter 16). We contacted likely manufacturers and were able to negotiate a contract with a leading company to develop the product for us, to manufacture it to our specifications, and to give us the exclusive right to distribute the product *under our brand* for at least five years. Just the process of envisioning, thinking, strategizing, and talking resulted in the mobilization of powerful physical resources! I conclude that even the ability to negotiate is a resource.

Financial Resources

From the day that you commit to building your business, you are destined to be absorbed in mobilizing, allocating, controlling, and generating this most crucial resource. Your venture will need money at *every* stage of its evolution, from start-up to maturity. If your business is doing well, you will need working capital for growth. If your business is in trouble, you will need money to regroup and restructure. Raising financial resources will be explored in greater detail in Chapter 17.

Knowledge Resources

Knowledge resources encompass many topics: patents, proprietary know-how, unique processes, research and development capabilities, the ability to invent, access to contract researchers, access to licensable technology, and creative ways of employing existing technology to give you competitive advantages. Proprietary knowledge confers a competitive advantage that rivals will be hard-pressed to copy—at least in the short term. Like you, your rivals can run down to the bank and get a loan. They can lease office space and equipment that is just like yours. They can hire manufacturers' representatives who are just as competent and aggressive as yours. But they cannot easily reproduce the proprietary know-how that makes your business special. If yours is a service business, clients will hire you because you understand something that they do not know how to do. Whether it's keeping company intranet servers working, designing a first-class web site, or knowing how to bake the most mouth-watering pastries, your knowledge is a key business resource. Develop it. Protect it.

Infrastructure Resources

This was one resource category that I neglected in my past entrepreneurial ventures. I just didn't pay enough attention to the basic underlying sub-structure of the business. I now understand the importance of up-to-date computer networks, information technology, communication systems, software programs, wireless capabilities, manuals for operations, quality control, purchasing, and personnel, to name but a few of the underlying support services. Productivity, efficiency, professionalism, and profits suffer without effective infrastructure.

Imagination Resources

Liberate the power of your own imagination. What other resources can move you faster and further? Depending on your business, they might be access to the marketplace through distribution channels, access to international markets, a recognized brand, access to door openers of all kinds, strategic partners, key customers, key suppliers, key support services (marketing, advertising, publicity firms, tool makers, subcontractors), stakeholders, strategic advisors, directors, core competencies of all kinds, your ability to negotiate, your strategic business plan as a living document and people-who-know-people-who-know-people resources.

One example: Frederick Gillis III, a successful financial advisor and entrepreneur from Boston, knows how to use imaginative resources in the pursuit of opportunity. Gillis noticed that hog farming in the Midwest had profit potential under the right conditions. The operations are complex, timing is crucial, and many things need to go right. His solution was to mobilize an alliance of partners, service providers, and physical facilities. Through contacts from national clients, he developed long-distance relationships with a feed mill, a veterinarian, a facilities manager, and a risk manager. Today, Gillis turns over 70,000 hogs annually from a distance of 2,000 miles (www .wholekranberryland.com). There are no limitations for the imaginative, resourceful entrepreneur!

Figure 14.3   Milestones for Purchase of Investment Property

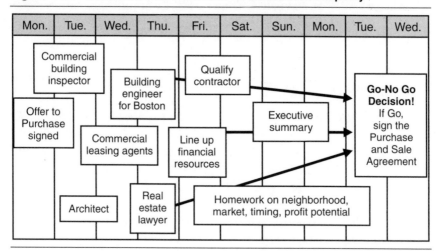

Source: www.CompetitiveSuccess.com, "Milestones for Purchase of Investment Property." Copyright © 2004 by Michael E. Gordon. Used with permission.

How to Mobilize Your Needed Resources

Whenever I am on an entrepreneurial scent, my starting point is to create a Milestone Chart. Recall that I had signed an Offer to Purchase Agreement, and I needed to mobilize resources quickly to reach a decision within 10 days about whether to sign the Purchase and Sale Agreement. Timing was very short, but fortunately I am good at mobilizing resources.

Look at Figure 14.3. This Milestone Chart enabled me to visualize what needed to happen and when. From this vantage point, I went on to create a detailed list of specific resources to reach each milestone. My phone, computer, and feet were humming as I mobilized all the necessary resources.

Summary

Entrepreneurial resources are anything that can move your venture further and faster and with the least risk, while improving your chance of success. In this chapter, we discussed the six categories of resources: people, physical, financial, knowledge, infrastructure, and imagination. Mobilizing resources should be one of the first things you think of as you pursue your entrepreneurial goal.

Actions

✓ Now it's your turn. Create your own milestone charts for the first month and year of your venture.

✓ Develop an action plan to mobilize needed resources. What? When? How? Think big, and outside the box. Don't be constrained by what you own. Chapter 17 teaches you about raising money.

✓ Now, go out and get them. Take action. Pick up the phone; set up a meeting; get in your car; do something RESOURCEFUL!

15

DEVELOP A SIMPLE,
EFFECTIVE BUSINESS PLAN

No journey of any consequence begins without a plan. The same applies to starting and operating your business. If you want to get where you intend to go, you need a road map. Without it, the outcome of all your labors will be strictly random—and probably disappointing. A business plan is generally a lengthy document and the product of a great deal of research and effort. At this point, however, you don't need a complete business plan; a miniplan—an executive summary—is enough to get you going. This chapter provides you with three things you need to develop your own executive summary:

1. An executive summary outline.
2. An example of a well-written executive summary.
3. A 10-point self-critique.

The recipe is here; all you need are your ingredients and draftsmanship.

By way of definition, the business plan[1] is just what it says: It is the complete plan, the road map, the blueprint for the start-up and growth of your business. It could be 30 to 50 pages in length and require considerable effort and research to develop. The body of the plan (about 25 pages) should discuss the following topics:

- Company description: products and services
- Industry dynamics
- Customer analysis
- Competitor analysis
- Strategy for gaining competitive advantages
- Marketing and sales plan
- Manufacturing and operations
- Product development
- Management team
- Business design
- Five-year financial projections (with assumptions)
- Funding needed
- Use of funds
- Keys to success and critical risks
- Milestones and schedule
- A 10- to 20-page appendix of supporting materials

An executive summary, on the other hand, presents the essence of your business in a concise, abstracted form—*four pages*. There are numerous reasons for having an executive summary:

- It tells *you* about the important aspects of the business you are creating. It forces you to tell the story to yourself, without hype or salesmanship, thereby helping you to make a go/no-go decision.
- It improves your chances of success by compelling you to look beyond the idea/opportunity to resource requirements, competition, market forces, revenue models, financial projections, and implementation.
- It allows the first substantive communication between you and your banker and potential investors. Even if you believe that you won't need outside investors, you yourself are the major investor of time, money, and energy. (*And you will need money.*)
- It is a vehicle for communicating your vision to your team, to door openers, and to other stakeholders.
- It permits you to think and get feedback about whether your vision is right-sized—or too small or too grand at this point in time. For example, are you projecting sales of $100,000 at the end of

five years, or $50 million? Can your assumptions support your projections?

- It is a living document that can evolve as you learn more about the validity of your assumptions.

When should you write your executive summary? NOW! As soon as you have put your idea through the opportunity screening funnel (Figure 6.2), start crafting your executive summary. Sooner is better than later, because it will help you to gain a 360° viewpoint of your own venture.

The outline that follows will assist you in organizing your thoughts when you create your executive summary. As you do so, put yourself in the shoes of a potential investor. Investors are very savvy and know how to scrutinize a deal on its merits, so be objective and avoid hype. Your job is to give them the information they need to make a decision—a decision in favor of your business.

In general, investors will look for nine points in an executive summary:

1. The uniqueness of the opportunity.
2. The value you will add for customers.
3. The business design, tying strategy, operations, and revenue streams together.
4. The time to reach breakeven sales.
5. The power and credibility of the founding entrepreneur and the team.
6. Sustainable competitive advantages.
7. Market dynamics, competition, and market penetration.
8. Credible assumptions and financial projections.
9. The keys to success and critical risks.

The information you present will give them a sense of the potential return on their investment, as well as the potential risks. All data and assumptions should be believable and verifiable. Everything will be revealed in any case when investors perform due diligence.[2] Due diligence is the inspection process that potential investors will go through to fully understand your venture. They will study every aspect of your business under a high-powered microscope. So don't make any statement that will not stand up to scrutiny.

As you construct your executive summary, include only the essential topics. If your venture is not technology based or operationally intensive, those sections should be excluded. Make sure that the unique aspects of your business are discussed at length. Pay considerable attention to your competition in your geographic market, and to your financial projections. Spell out *why* your business will succeed.

Finally, make sure that your summary reflects high professional standards, with correct grammar and spelling and attention to detail. Make your summary clear, concise, and comprehensive. Above all, *make it compelling!* Investors see many executive summaries and business plans in the course of the typical month. Yours must stand out from the crowd.

By writing your executive summary for investors, you are really telling the story to yourself.

EXECUTIVE SUMMARY OUTLINE AND SUBTOPICS

The Company and Concept

This is where you introduce your idea. Be brief, be precise, and be interesting.

- Describe clearly what business you are in. Use diagrams to clarify your concept, if needed.
- Communicate the excitement and the urgency of the story, without hype.
- Describe the essence of your product or service line.

Mission Statement

Specify your business position and geographic domain in 1 or 2 sentences. Make it short and compelling.

Example: "To emerge as the dominant provider of wireless extranet services by commercializing our breakthrough technology aimed at small to midsize businesses throughout the world."

Opportunity

How you describe your business opportunity is very important (reread Chapter 6). Explain why this is a unique opportunity for customers, and why it would thereby be attractive to investors. An investment-worthy opportunity addresses the following issues:

- There is unique value that you add for your customers.
- Your product or service is feasible and achievable.
- There is a timely window of opportunity.
- There are one or more points of competitive advantage.
- There are hungry, needy customers who are not being served.
- There is the potential for high profit margins.
- The concept is durable and sustainable—not a one-shot deal.
- The opportunity came from changing circumstances, new technology, nagging problems, or the confluence of two or more situations.
- The concept is disruptive to your competitors.
- The industry is attractive in growth potential, size, and your ability to gain market share.

Core Technology

If yours is a technology venture, you will need to include the following details:

- Describe the technology in sufficient detail. Don't reveal proprietary or crucial information.
- Describe how you came to own the technology.
- Define its sustainability and barriers to future competitors through patent protection or proprietary know-how.
- If the technology is licensed, explain the exclusiveness of the license.
- Describe your contributions to the development of this technology. Mention any unique research and development capabilities you have.

Competition

It is important to show potential investors that you have analyzed your competition and have a strategy to gain advantage (refer to Chapters 8 and 12).

- Analyze the industry dynamics: buyers, suppliers, substitutes, new entrants, intensity of competitive rivalry.
- Describe and compare *all* major competitors. Often, an entrepreneur will claim there are no competitors. That might imply there is no existing market, that there are no present buyers, no future competitors, and no substitutes.

- Define your competitive advantages in detail.
- Anticipate the competitors' responses to your entry. Don't underestimate their reactions.

Market Penetration Strategy

Potential investors will be looking for evidence that you thoroughly understand your market and how to gain market share (refer to Chapter 12).

- Define your customers and how you will reach them.
- Quantify the size, growth rate, and other characteristics of your industry.
- Explain your market penetration strategy: alliances, distributors, direct salespeople, mail order, franchising, multilevel marketing, Internet, sales representatives, or dealers that can promote your products.

The Team

The executive summary is one place to sell yourself to investors. But you must also sell the team that will be making their (your) investment dreams come true.

- Mention specific pertinent skills, entrepreneurial accomplishments, and industry track record that will lead to your company's future success.
- Discuss your plans to build a self-sustaining organization.

Present Status

Here is the place to highlight your track record:

- Describe the history of the company to the present.
- List significant accomplishments and milestones achieved.
- Present a snapshot of your company today.

Operations

If investors will need to understand the operational details of this opportunity, discuss them here:

- Explain how your company delivers goods and performs services.
- Describe any unique manufacturing or supply capabilities.
- Describe your present space, facilities, and infrastructure.

Business Design

Your business design defines how you convert your opportunity into money and customer satisfaction. It ties together operations, revenue streams, and strategy (refer to Chapter 9):

- Delineate who your customers are: consumers, businesses, value-added resellers, distributors, dealers, or third parties of any kind.
- Discuss in quantitative terms how much money you make per transaction.
- Discuss specific pricing strategies, volume discounts, distributor pricing, finders' and brokers' fees.
- Explain any innovative methods you have for delivering your product or service to the customer.

Financial Projections

It is very important to quantify how and when this opportunity is going to make money for your investors (refer to Chapter 13):

- Define the key assumptions on which you have built your financial projections.
- Detail your five-year income projections.
- Identify breakeven sales and time to reach positive cash flow.

Future Growth and Developments

Finally, describe where and how you will take your company into the future:

- Describe your strategies for growth.
- Talk about staged introduction of other products.
- Discuss internal growth plans: marketing, product development, licensing, franchising, other company-owned stores, international distribution opportunities.

- Describe external growth plans: strategic alliances, acquisitions, mergers.
- Mention plans you may have for vertical integration.
- Address plans for diversification into new businesses.

Tip: An appropriate format is four full pages (*not longer*), in Times New Roman, 11 point, with one-inch margins all around and single-spaced.

Suggestion: Pause here; mark this page and check off the sections that must go into your own executive summary before you go on to the example. There isn't room for everything. Be selective. What must potential investors know as an introduction to your venture?

EXAMPLE OF AN EXECUTIVE SUMMARY

The Beading Café[3]
Executive Summary

January 2007

The Company

The Beading Café is a new company that will provide a community environment for avid bead lovers of all skill levels. Located in Brookline Village, the Company will offer regular and frequent classes and will sell a comprehensive array of beads from around the world, tools, findings, supplies, and finished beaded jewelry from our own inventory and on consignment.

Our value proposition for our customers is based on the creation of a magnetic, aesthetic, friendly atmosphere. Repeat customers will come for the camaraderie, for the learning experience, and to create their own beautiful beadwork. In a gracious 1,500-square-foot setting, supplies and work tables will be available, in addition to continuous free tea, honey, mint, and lemon. Sandwiches, salads, gourmet coffees, pastries, and other snacks will be available for sale. Skilled teachers will be retained on an as-needed basis. When classes are not being held, videos will be shown so that regular customers can learn on their own as they purchase the needed supplies. There will be background music for aesthetics. The company will expand through acquisitions, new stores, and franchises.

Our Mission

To build a very profitable chain of beading stores based on a social, creative, learning atmosphere.

Keys to Success

- Implementing a winning concept based on a magnetic culture of camaraderie, beading, and aesthetics.
- Marketing, marketing, marketing, marketing, marketing.
- Capturing very desirable locations and expanding through acquisitions, starting new stores, and franchising.
- Mobilizing financial resources for new locations.

Market Characteristics

The retail beading business is a regional and fragmented market. Competition is local, and there are no dominant branded beading competitors. Our first store will be located in Brookline Village; there are 9 other beading stores in our geographic market (within a radius of 10 miles). What is missing in this attractive and profitable beading market is the social community environment. As the first mover, we will have a short-term advantage. Other competitors will be able to copy our best practices and to replicate our concept. However, through an aggressive local advertising and promotion program, we intend to capture market share quickly. Once captured, the customers will be ours, and we will not take them for granted.

Competition

Competitors	Location	Social	Supplies	Classes	Cafe
The Beading Café	Brookline	Yes	Yes	Yes	Yes
Bead Company of America	Cambridge,	No	Yes	Yes	No
	Boston	No	Yes	Yes	No
Red Crystal	Watertown	No	Yes	Yes	No
Beads Boston	Newton	No	Yes	No	No
Beautiful Creations	Winthrop	No	Yes	No	No
Ancient Stars	Watertown	No	Yes	No	No
Belle Art Supplies	Newton	No	Yes	No	No
Rose Garden	Brookline	No	Yes	No	No
Bini's Tree House	Boston	No	Yes	No	No
Personal Jewels	Cambridge	No	Yes	No	No

The Team

The Company has a strong management team of two seasoned beading enthusiasts with extensive experience in and knowledge of the beading business:

Alejandra Figaredo, CEO, brings extensive aesthetic and operational experience to this present position, as well as 15 years as a beading hobbyist. She worked as part-time supervisor in a jewelry store in Houston for three years and understands the operations and supply chain. She has run beading classes in her home for the past six years and has developed advanced beading skills. Her entrepreneurial enthusiasm and deep background will enable her to build this chain of beading stores.

Andrea Sandras, vice president of marketing, is an accomplished jewelry artist. Her passion is to design, make, and sell unique jewelry from precious metals, minerals, and beads. Her marketing skills have enabled her to establish a consignment arts and crafts business locally and over the Internet that has been profitable for many years.

Financial Projections (All Financial Numbers in $000)

	2007	2008	2009	2010	2011
Total number of locations	1	1	1	2	3
Revenue streams					
Product sales ($K)	110	180	320	500	650
Classes	30	60	80	120	250
Food/Beverages	40	80	100	230	300
Total revenue	180	320	500	850	1,200
Cost of goods sold	90	160	250	425	600
Earnings from operations	8	36	55	94	140
Financing needs	100	—	—	200	250

(Don't get nervous. Review Chapter 13.)

Investment Summary

Several factors have resulted in an attractive opportunity for The Beading Café:

- *The management team* is strong, motivated, and experienced. Both partners bring operational, marketing, and artistic talent to the business.
- *Revenues* will come from four sources: supplies, classes, food, and Internet sales.

- *Profits will grow* as other locations are opened, franchised, or acquired. Higher profits will result from economies of scale for inventory, as well as from franchisee royalties and uniform financial and operational control systems.
- *Timeliness:* No competitor has emerged to fill this niche for a social and aesthetic beading café environment.

The Beading Café

302 Cary Ave., Brookline, MA 02020
Tel: (617) 890-XXXX Fax: (617) 890-YYYY
www.TheBeadingCafe.com

Suggestion: Pause here, mark this page, and consider the strengths and weaknesses of this document. Now begin to actually outline your own executive summary. Which of these concepts can you use in the development of your executive summary as you go on to the 10-Point Self-Critique?

Your Executive Summary: A 10-Point Self-Critique[4]

Review your summary from the perspective of a seasoned investor. As you do so, rate the desirability of your deal objectively in each category as *excellent, good, fair,* or *poor.* Circle your choices.

1. Return on Investment

Excellent—Good—Fair—Poor

Investors in early-stage deals want significant returns for their invested risk capital, typically 5 to 10 times their investment in 5 to 7 years. This may seem high, but remember that 80 percent of venture capital portfolio companies don't make it all the way to harvest.

For there to be an attractive return on investment, the present valuation must be appropriately low compared to the future valuation at harvest.

For there to be a return on investment, there must be a liquidation event, or harvest. This implies that the venture survived and thrived for a minimum of 5 to 7 years, leading to an acquisition, a merger, or an initial public offering. (Refer to Chapter 17.)

2. Is the Venture Concept a Compelling Opportunity?

Excellent—Good—Fair—Poor

A central theme in entrepreneurship is that there is a world of difference between an idea and an opportunity. Less than five percent of all venture ideas are potential opportunities. So what are the characteristics of an opportunity? An opportunity creates unique, differentiated value for your customer; it is feasible and achievable; it is timely; it has durable, competitive advantages; it is market driven—there are hungry/needy customers who will pay dearly for your product or service, resulting in high gross profit margins; there is a strong likelihood that your venture will become a positive Money Machine soon; there will be a harvest in the 5- to 7-year time frame. You are clearly differentiated from the herd of competitors.

3. Is This a Lifestyle or High-Potential Venture?

Excellent—Good—Fair—Poor

A lifestyle venture is a business that will create a job and a lifestyle for the founding entrepreneur. This business will be slower growing, small (under $1 million in sales), and localized. A high-potential venture, on the other hand, might be projected to grow to $10 million or more in a 5- to 7-year time frame. Do not concern yourself if your venture has the characteristics of a lifestyle business. The vast majority of businesses in the world are lifestyle. They have managed to get funding and to survive. Furthermore, it is not unusual for lifestyle businesses to grow into high-potential ventures. As a lifestyle entrepreneur, you will still require an executive summary to communicate with lenders, team members, all other potential stakeholders, *and with yourself.*

4. Are the CEO and the Team Able to Create Success?

Excellent—Good—Fair—Poor

Investors will look very closely at the credibility of the CEO and the team. Their skills and character traits will be the subtext of all funding discussions. Desirable skills and traits include maturity, passion, opportunity obsession, balanced perspective, commitment to success, leadership ability, pertinent experience, frugality, absence of exaggeration, adaptability, listening skills, ability to orchestrate win-win negotiations, and ethics.

Individual entrepreneurs tend to create lifestyle ventures; teams create high-potential ventures. Move in the direction of identifying and bringing in the best people to build your venture with you. Emphasize team strength and a winning mentality. During the due diligence process, investors will seek to understand the strength and synergy of your team.

5. How Soon Will Operating Cash Flow Be Positive?

Excellent—Good—Fair—Poor

This is very important! Investors do not want to have their equity position diluted for the wrong reasons, such as distributing stock options/warrants frivolously to future investors and employees; too much time in product development; lack of frugality; and false starts with the design of the Money Machine. When is investor dilution acceptable? When the company is growing so rapidly that working capital, inventory, marketing, and human resources must be increased.

6. Are There Barriers Slowing Down the Competition?

Excellent—Good—Fair—Poor

In this category are competitive advantages, patents and other intellectual property protection, proprietary knowledge, access to money and other essential resources, access to distribution channels, and core competencies not available to competitors.

7. Are the Market Dynamics Favorable?

Excellent—Good—Fair—Poor

Analyze the following market issues:

a. Is your market niche large enough to accommodate your projected growth? Simply stated, you cannot grow a $20 million venture within a $10 million total market segment.
b. Is the market itself growing rapidly, or must you take market share from your competitors? This is challenging, but possible.
c. Are there many fragmented, small competitors, or are there a few dominant competitors?
d. Are the customers easily identified and reachable through your marketing program?

8. Are Financial Assumptions and Projections Credible?

Excellent—Good—Fair—Poor

You have an uphill task to convince investors of the validity of your assumptions and financial projections. They will assume that you have overstated the revenue projections by a factor of 2+, understated the operating costs by a factor of 2+, and underestimated the time to market and time to breakeven by a factor of 2+. Define your assumptions meticulously. You can establish your credibility by *validation* of your business model through satisfied customers who have actually purchased and reordered products. If this is not possible, perform market surveys by talking to potential customers. Understand the effects of revenue increases or decreases and operating cost increases or decreases on operating cash flow. Perform a detailed breakeven analysis that can stand up to investor scrutiny (review Chapter 13).

9. Is There an Astute Market Penetration Strategy?

Excellent—Good—Fair—Poor

In the market that you intend to penetrate, there are already buyers and suppliers. All customers that need/want your product are currently being supplied by your existing competitors. How will you reach potential buyers and convince them to switch allegiance to you? For starters, you need to be different! Your products or services need to have customer-valued uniqueness. Think outside the box. Are there one or two killer penetration strategies that will establish your position in the marketplace?

10. Is the Executive Summary Professional?

Excellent—Good—Fair—Poor

Look over the entire document objectively and consider its appearance and the flow and style of the writing. Avoid vagueness, imprecision, and speculation. Have you done extensive research? You do not want to be in the untenable position of knowing less about your venture than the potential investors.

SUMMARY

In this chapter, you have learned how to create your executive summary and to evaluate your own opportunity before you begin to spend money.

Using the investor's looking glass, you have gained an unbiased view of your business.

Actions

√ Now it is time to develop your own executive summary. No matter how rough it is, don't leave this chapter without something in hand. Guesstimate. Just start writing!

√ Using your executive summary, make practice presentations (15 minutes each) to family, friends, advisors—anyone who will listen. Keep your mind wide open to their responses, and solicit wholesome input.

√ Revise and upgrade your executive summary as you learn from each meeting. As your executive summary evolves, you will know its strengths and weaknesses completely. And this is what you want to accomplish.

√ Next, make a presentation to your banker. You are not meeting with him or her necessarily to borrow money, but to get more sophisticated feedback and to begin a banking relationship. You will also appreciate how, why, and under what conditions bankers lend money.

√ With all that you have learned, make a reasoned decision whether to proceed with this particular opportunity, to collect more information, or to go back in search of other ideas and opportunities. This is a critical juncture.

Pep Talk

Nicely done! This was not easy. The hours you have spent on your executive summary have been well worth the effort. By learning to see your business through the seasoned eyes of investors, you have improved your own chance and magnitude of success.

16

BECOME A
WIN-WIN NEGOTIATOR

In my business career, I have made a small fortune by studying and applying the principles of win-win negotiation. *Now, that is the ultimate Money Machine!* I was able to create significant wealth by envisioning, thinking, strategizing, and talking. By understanding what goes on in the process of negotiation, I also increased my chances of succeeding. I didn't feel unarmed when dealing with more experienced and powerful players, and I was able to prevent exploitation by being more prepared.

In this chapter, I share with you some general principles of negotiation[1]—win-win negotiation, in particular—and illustrate these with an example. By the end of the chapter, you will also have learned 20 positional negotiating techniques that you can apply to every aspect of your business, in dealing with suppliers, employees, customers, investors, and so on. Hopefully, what you learn here will whet your appetite for more on this crucial subject. This topic is especially timely because our next chapter is about raising money. Your knowledge of the negotiating process will be essential as you seek investors.

In business, give-and-take exchanges go on constantly: My partner and I need to agree on an urgent issue; an employee wants a raise or more benefits; a supplier wants higher prices; a customer wants lower prices; the

Photo courtesy of the Trump Organization.

 ## Negotiating with Donald Trump and His Organization

Imagine this: You are an entrepreneur with a truly bold vision for a new business unit that would benefit greatly if you could leverage the Trump brand. You develop an executive summary and rehearse your presentation. With dogged persistence, you make contact with one of the executives in the Trump Organization who screens new business opportunities. To your joy, you have captured his interest, and he arranges a meeting between you and Donald Trump. Fifteen minutes—not one minute more! Mr. Trump is interested and tells you to come back for a second 15-minute meeting when you have a full business plan. The second meeting results in a decision to GO. But a go is not a go. Now you had better be a skillful negotiator. For months you will be negotiating with some of the toughest dealmakers in the Trump Organization, with legal, business, and financial skills. For starters, they will present you with a term sheet containing several nonnegotiable points. Beyond that, the negotiation process will span the range from "big picture" to haggling. You will be tested to your limits. Where is your boundary? When will you walk away? Negotiating with the Trump Organization will be one of the most exciting and challenging things that will happen to you in life. At the end of the process, it will be either win-win, or no deal at all. A deal only works if both parties are happy!

bank wants higher interest rates; I want to raise money from private investors, but under more favorable conditions; the landlord wants more favorable terms for renewal of our lease. The bargaining process never ends. And each interaction needs to result in a productive, wholesome, and *continuing* relationship.

Business isn't the only arena in which negotiating skills are essential. In personal relationships, the bargaining process is also ongoing: Your spouse wants to vacation in Cancun, but you want to go to France. Your children want a dog, but you know that the dog will be your responsibility. Cousin Barbara borrowed your car and totaled it; how will you settle up? You and your brother inherited equally a beautiful piece of sculpture, and each of you wants to own it entirely. And on and on.

Each person in a personal or business relationship has needs and wants that must be fulfilled in such a way that both parties feel satisfied, to the extent possible. Accomplishing this requires trade-offs, accommodations, taking less, giving more, in an effort to find an acceptable balance among all issues. And the complexities increase exponentially when there are more than two parties involved.

The common theme in all of this is the desire and need for a continuing, mutually satisfying relationship between parties, and that is where win-win negotiation comes in.[2] If you and I reach agreement in a win-win manner, then you are happy, and *you are happy that I am happy*; I am happy, and *I am happy that you are happy*. Now that is a lot of happiness, and that is the basis for a truly abundant relationship going forward. Success in life and in business depends on your ability to negotiate these mutually beneficial outcomes, to work out disagreements, to mediate, to solve problems together, and to reach harmony.

Relationship builders first seek to understand what the other person needs and wants, and then figure out how to reach mutually agreeable accommodations. Each party works hard to leave emotions at the door when trying to reach solutions. They disassociate the individual personalities from the specific challenges at hand and use impartial standards to seek a fair solution. Then they act as partners to brainstorm creative ways to reach agreement, and to compromise, so that each party is pleased with the outcome. This is what win-win negotiation is all about. The perfect example of this principle is when you are negotiating with a potential investor for a percentage ownership in your company. If the deal goes to completion successfully, your negotiating opponent becomes your business partner— for the long term. You can readily see the advantages of approaching negotiations with win-win as the goal.

If there is to be no continuing relationship, as in the case when you horse-trade over an antique picture (of a horse, of course) at a flea market, then win-win negotiation has no role. You make your best deal and walk away forever. What you gain or win because of your haggling ability results directly in less profit for the seller. You might call this a win-lose negotiation. The other end of the spectrum is when you and the seller cannot reach agreement and both parties lose; you both wanted to do the deal but could not find the point of equilibrium, resulting in a lose-lose situation. A lose-lose result is not usually a problem when there is to be no continuing relationship. You didn't buy the antique horse picture; so be it. The problem comes when there are needs and wants for a continuing relationship, and then nagging dissatisfaction sets in. In fact, every strained relationship, whether business or personal, is caused by unresolved expectations, wants, and needs. And that does not work for long. Seeking a win-win result is the only solution.

THE 50/50 PARTNER

By way of example, let me share with you one noteworthy example from many negotiations that I have lived through. It was resolved successfully in a win-win fashion.

Years ago, I was in a service business in partnership with an older man, 25 years my senior. We had grown to be friends over the years. For personal reasons, I wanted to sell my 50 percent interest in the company and realized that there would be only one possible buyer: my partner. It was not the type of business that anyone else would want without having a controlling interest. Usually, in a 50/50 partnership, major decisions have to be made by agreement between both partners. If there are disagreements, the company can get bogged down, without an easy method of resolution. I approached my partner to initiate discussions about his buying my share, but he expressed little interest. Over the next few months, I continued to surface the discussion. Finally, he expressed a lukewarm willingness to buy me out for half of the company's net worth (Chapter 13), which was 10 percent of what I believed the business was truly worth. After all, it was an operating company that had been in business for many years and had been continuously generating modest profits. I had a very limited understanding of negotiation and felt powerless. What could I do?

I was determined not to give the business away to my partner for a fraction of its worth. Worse yet, there would be taxes, legal fees, and accounting fees on the sale. For the next four months, I diligently studied the art of negotiation and developed a solid working knowledge of this empowering subject. As I read about the subtleties of negotiation, I would seek out opportunities to practice. Two months later, my partner bought my share of the business at a price 50 percent *greater* than my original target value. And we both got what we really wanted. How could a win-win result have emerged from this one-sided hardball game?

First, I had to get his attention by also playing serious hardball, and then to coach him on the art of being a win-win player. According to the teachings of negotiation, I had to figure out what my partner really wanted in life and in this transaction, and balance that with my own wants. With that as a starting point, I could then put together a strategy to encourage him to see the situation differently and to lead us out of stalemate. One day, my attention was captured by a large, magnificent family painting hanging on the wall behind his desk. He and his wife were in the center, surrounded by their three children, their children's spouses, their grandchildren—even the family dog. He was the patriarch, and his family was his legacy. *And then I knew!* He really did want to own the entire business, but he wanted to pay a bargain-basement price. As there could be no other buyer but him, he believed he had time to wait.

My next discussion with my partner went like this:

> Partner, having known you for many years, I appreciate how much you care for your family, and for their well-being into the far future. Your family portrait speaks volumes about your loving, protective nature. The safekeeping of your family is your legacy. I am offering you an unprecedented opportunity to own our whole company. Someday, your children and grandchildren might want to work in the business. For my part, I cannot sell the company to you at a fraction of its net worth, so that I would retain my 50 percent ownership without working in the company. You would then be working for me, because we would share the profits equally, as equal partners. There could be no undeclared dividends, second cars, vacations, inappropriate bonuses, and benefits. Frankly speaking, if you were to die suddenly, your estate would then have to negotiate with me and sell your share of the business at a fraction of its net worth.

I suggested that he consider my offer as an opportunity for us both to benefit. If he wished to move forward with the acquisition, we would use objective criteria to value the business, and we could brainstorm mutually agreeable options for financing and other issues. As I mentioned earlier, the deal closed successfully; we each were satisfied with the terms; we remained good friends, and our amiable relationship continued.

THE FIVE PHASES OF THE NEGOTIATION PROCESS

What went on during the negotiation just described? Generally, I've found that successful win-win negotiations go through five phases.

Phase 1: Establish the Vision

What are the results I want to accomplish, specifically and quantitatively? In the first example, my vision was to sell my 50 percent share of the company to my partner within six months for a fair or better price. I also wanted our friendship to continue after the sale. Additionally, there would be many other legal conditions that needed to be resolved to complete the sale. I now believe that the best way to develop my vision statement is for me to actually write a first draft of the ideal contract (in abstract form, this would be known as the term sheet), one that is reasonable and yet favorable to me. Having this optimal document shows me the total scope of our agreement-to-be. By sharing this road map with my negotiating counterpart, we have a starting point for our discussions. In business, I believe that strong relationships are built on meticulously clear contracts.

Phase 2: Plan to Succeed

This is the homework stage, where I needed to gain essential expertise and devise a strategy. Many questions must be asked and answered:

- With whom am I really negotiating? In the example, my partner's wife was a strong influencing factor on his decisions. Certainly his lawyer and accountant were also influencing him.
- Who has the power, and what is the nature of the power imbalance? At first, my partner believed that he had the power because there was only one buyer: him.
- What is my strategy? My strategy needed to focus on reversing his perception of the balance of power in my favor. Otherwise, I would not have a chance of reaching my vision.
- What was really important to my partner? He very much wanted to own the entire business at a fraction of its worth. He viewed the business as a means of providing for the financial well-being of his family. He wanted to buy cheap.

- What was really important to me? This was fully defined in the draft agreement that I created. The essence was to sell at a fair or better price within six months.
- What should my expectations be for all significant conditions of the final agreement? This is where homework comes in. I had to learn how to place a value on the business—the lowest, the highest, and the most likely, based on objective criteria. There were many other conditions in the sections on payment, default, noncompetition, confidentiality, warranties, representations, and so on. (Don't worry about the details for now. But you certainly need to know what the lawyers are going to add later on.)
- Who has the higher level of desire and desperation to complete the deal? And how can I lower my desire and increase my partner's desperation? In this example, I indicated that if the price were too low, I would continue to own 50 percent of the business without working and that he would be generating profits for me. I also pointed out the issues if he were to die suddenly (remember, he was 25 years my senior).
- Anticipate what will cause stalemate (getting stuck) and brainstorm possible win-win solutions around these roadblocks *beforehand*. Role-play with knowledgeable advisors.

Phase 3: Use Winning Language and Winning Techniques

In all negotiations (win-win or not), it is *always* necessary to face off on key issues. This is called positional negotiation (or haggling), and the likelihood and magnitude of your success can be enhanced dramatically through knowledge and practice. Twenty positional negotiating techniques are listed in Exhibit 16.1.

Phase 4: Unblock Stalemate

Every complex negotiation *will* go into stalemate on one or more critical issues. A stalemate is the condition (hopefully temporary) of impasse, where the parties cannot reach agreement on one or more issues and the negotiation gets stuck. I view stalemate as a positive opportunity to form a strong partnership with the other side, and at the same time, to test the boundaries of the deal. It is the time to focus on interests rather than positions and to use principles of fairness and objectivity to move forward. It is the

1	**Create a friendly atmosphere:** Use a slow and gentle approach; build a relationship first; use humor to diffuse difficult situations. Build trust through openness and straightforwardness.
2	**Allow your opponent to establish the first baseline:** You might reject her first baseline based on unacceptability. Encourage her to lower her baseline, even before you begin to negotiate.
3	**Insert your baseline gently:** If it is embarrassingly low, you will lose respect as a serious negotiating partner. The negotiation could end here if you are not careful and reasonable.
4	**Justify your baseline** with information, facts, and reason. Show other similar transactions and comparable values. Be prepared to counter any negotiating points that contradict your goals.
5	**Convince him that your intentions are serious:** You are a reasonable negotiator and seek a fair, mutually beneficial deal. But the deal has to make sense.
6	**Encourage her to lower her baseline even further:** This might be the time to discuss the limits of what you are and are not prepared to do. And why. Solid reasons have power.
7	**Pause, think, and use time as an ally:** Do not be rushed into a change of position. Express understanding, and delay your decision. As you back off, you will have an opportunity to understand his desire.
8	**Move away from your baseline slowly:** Show flexibility without making major concessions quickly. Small, incremental increases show a willingness to accommodate.
9	**Use competition to your advantage:** Other buyers or sellers are waiting around the corner to do this deal. If the deal does not go through, you are prepared to wait for the right buyer/seller.
10	**Use the possibility of stalemate to your advantage:** What is really going on is that each party is testing the boundaries of stuck positions. This can be productive, but be careful.
11	**"No" is an answer** (temporarily): If the other side makes a proposal that is unacceptable to you, you can refuse based on reason, fairness, and objectivity. Remember: friendly and gentle.
12	**Splitting the difference is not necessary:** "I have made a sincere offer; it is the best I can do; splitting the difference would not be fair."

Exhibit 16.1   Continued

13	**Avoid take-it-or-leave-it positions:** I will (almost) never accept or use the take-it-or-leave-it ploy. If at all possible, I will leave it, because my opponent is playing hardball and not seeking win-win.
14	**Reinforce his desire to complete the deal:** In the 50/50 partner example, I gave him reasons why it was important for *him* to conclude this deal on my terms.
15	**The total deal must be acceptable**, even though it is negotiated in pieces. Reserve the right to make changes at the end. Even if you have reached agreement, sometimes it is necessary to reopen.
16	**This for that:** Whenever you give something up, or compromise, ask for something in return. Be prepared. Anticipate what your negotiating counterpart may ask from you.
17	**Focus on mutual interests:** Avoid drawing lines in the sand over positions. Stalemate always occurs around stubborn positions. Keep searching for the mutual benefits of a successful deal.
18	**Set standards for fairness and objectivity:** Good negotiations are based on reasonableness and understanding of the other side. Be reasonable and insist on reasonableness in return.
19	**Brainstorm all options** with your negotiating partner to find a mutually acceptable compromise. Work hard; don't give up. This is the opportunity to cement a future win-win relationship.
20	**When negotiating with a counterpart from a different culture**, study the cultural perspective that the other party brings to the table. Without this cultural respect, the negotiation is likely to be doomed.

Source: www.CompetitiveSuccess.com, "Twenty Positional Negotiating Techniques." Copyright © 2000 by Michael E. Gordon. Used with permission. ***This exhibit can be downloaded from www.trumpuniversity.com/entrepreneurship101 for your personal use.***

time to show that you understand each other's viewpoints and to work hard to reach agreement through compromise.[3] This takes you in the direction of forming a healthy, long-term, working relationship. If the standoff becomes permanent, the negotiation is over (or you can think BABSON).

Phase 5: When All Else Fails, Think BABSON[4]

When I am in a negotiation that is just on the brink of permanent, intractable stalemate, I ask myself what is my:

B est
A lternative
B efore
S hutting
O ff
N egotiations

I may not be happy with one or two issues of the deal, but the real question is: Am I better or worse off if I accept this less-than-desirable total agreement? I owned a condominium in downtown Boston, for which I paid $154,000. The real estate market was weakening and I wanted to become liquid by selling the property. Another very attractive deal was waiting for me. A potential buyer was willing to pay $123,000, and not one penny more. We were locked in stalemate. I did not want to take a 20 percent loss, but by thinking BABSON, I took the offer, and then invested in the other deal. The new deal tripled in value within six years. (This is one of my favorite acronyms because I teach at Babson College.)

Summary

This chapter provides an overview of the principles of win-win and positional negotiation. This topic was selected from the list of 11 Essential Entrepreneurial Power Skills (Chapter 2) as one of the keys to your business and personal successes in life. The process of negotiation involves:

1. Establish your vision.
2. Plan to succeed.
3. Use winning language and techniques.
4. Unblock stalemate.
5. When all else fails, think BABSON.

Actions

√ Commit to learning the art of negotiation, particularly win-win negotiation. This will be one of your most valuable entrepreneurial tools.
√ Use every garage sale as an opportunity to practice. Even in win-win negotiation, one side has better negotiating skills and can shift the balance in his or her favor.
√ If you have business or social relationships that are not abundant, turn them around by educating your counterparts about win-win negotiation.

17

RAISE MONEY

Years ago, my banker recounted the parable of a naive young man who was determined to find his soul mate. Week after week, month after month, the young man would go to singles events, searching with eager anticipation for the woman of his dreams. Frustration mounted as time after time his hopes were dashed. The problem? He would show up unshaven, hair snarled, unwashed, poorly dressed, wrinkled, and odorous. In a word, he was unkempt. Worse still was that his shabby reputation would precede him to every singles event thereafter. I got the point.

My banker was letting me know not so subtly that my venture was unkempt, and that I should not try to raise capital until I cleaned up my act. "For starters, you need a funding plan," he told me.

A funding plan ties together six elements. In this chapter, you learn to:

1. Clarify your business goals.
2. Understand your money needs at each stage of growth.
3. Select appropriate sources of capital.
4. Improve your chances of equity investor interest.
5. Take the most likely path to early-stage funding.
6. Orchestrate the funding process.

Money is the fuel needed to get your venture onto the launchpad and then propel it into space. Prelaunch, you will need money to develop and market test your new product, to purchase an initial inventory, to pay for the first several months of office rent, to buy equipment, to pay salaries until cash starts rolling in, and so on. After liftoff, you will need working capital to fuel growth. Every business has different money needs at each stage of its growth.

The process of raising money for your business is difficult and time-consuming—especially for the first-time entrepreneur. The money hunt is also confusing due to the maze of funding sources, most of which have special requirements and terms. Without appropriate knowledge, you will be ill equipped to navigate the funding maze. To get through the difficulties and confusion, let's take it one manageable step at a time. The first step is to understand your own business goals.

CLARIFY YOUR BUSINESS GOALS

Look over the following four questions and craft a simple statement of your business goals, encompassing the size, nature, growth rate, and harvest.

1. *Do you want to grow a lifestyle business or a high-potential venture?* Recall from Chapter 6 that a lifestyle business can grow slowly, perhaps from $100,000 to $1 million in sales, and will provide a nice lifestyle for you, as your own boss. A high-potential venture has the capability of growing rapidly, perhaps in excess of $10 million in sales in a 5- to 10-year time frame.
2. *What is the nature of the company you wish to create:* products or services, marketing, sales, R&D, finance, virtual, international, manufacturing, distribution, retail, socially conscious, not-for-profit, others? Every company has a basic nature.
3. *How quickly do you want to grow?* Building a business in one industry, slowly, from profits? Rapidly, by taking in financing partners, by establishing a network of franchisees, by establishing other company-owned stores, through acquisitions or mergers?
4. *What is the most likely harvest scenario for your business?* Do you want to grow your company and sell it quickly, within 5 to 10 years, or work until retirement and turn it over to your children?

Your business goal statement will set the stage for finding and approaching well-suited investors. There must be congruence between your goals and those of the targeted funding source. By way of example, if you envision growing a computer consulting company having sales of $500,000 in five years, you would not approach a private investor who is interested in funding a rapid-growth chain of specialty foods to leverage his expertise in restaurant franchising and distribution. In fact, if you do not envision selling your company in the 5- to 10-year term, you would need to get quite creative to provide a return on investment to *any* equity partner. The greater the clarity of your business goals, the more likely is your chance of finding appropriate sources and getting funded. The goals of funding sources are described later. For now, let's explore the capital needs of your business.

UNDERSTAND YOUR MONEY NEEDS AT EACH PHASE OF GROWTH

You will need money at all phases of your company's growth, from concept to development, through start-up and beyond. If your business is doing well, you will need growth and working capital. If your company is struggling, you will need money to ride through difficult times. We touched on your financial needs in Chapter 3. Now, let's peel the onion and understand the specifics during each of the stages shown in Exhibit 17.1.

Concept Stage: From Idea to Opportunity: You are proactively searching for ideas, going to trade shows, attending networking meetings, taking how-to courses, meeting with business brokers, and then filtering likely opportunities through the Opportunity Screening Funnel (Chapters 5 and 6). When you do zero in on a potential opportunity, capital is needed for concept feasibility, proof of customer demand, sleuthing of competitors, validating and refining your business plan, prototype construction, and so on. You may need to hire an industry consultant to provide objective product testing.

Preproduction Stage: You have made the courageous decision to go forward. In this stage, you are readying your product or service for market, building your team, implementing your sales/marketing budget, and positioning your company to take its first order. Money will be required for inventory, infrastructure, equipment, space and utilities, travel, supplies, legal fees, and so on.

Zero Stage to Early Growth: Your needs for capital increase as you launch your venture. Working capital is needed to cover all fixed and

Stages of Growth and Categories of Financial Need	Minimum $ Needed	Maximum $$$ Needed
Concept Stage: From Idea to Opportunity 1. Proactive search for ideas/opportunities 2. Concept feasibility/prototype construction 3. Hardware/software development 4. Proof of customer need/demand 5. Sleuthing of competitors 6. Business plan development 7. Misc.: travel, consultants, contractors, ... Total $ Needs ⟶		
Decision to Go Forward: Yes / No		
Preproduction Stage 1. Readying product or service for market 2. Inventory—initial 3. Equipment 4. Space 5. People 6. Sales and marketing budget 7. Infrastructure—initial needs 8. Others: travel, supplies, legal, utilities ... Total $ Needs ⟶		
Zero Stage to Early Growth 1. Working capital 2. Building the organization 3. Increasing sales and marketing budgets 4. Space 5. Inventory 6. Infrastructure: computers, phones, systems, ... 7. All fixed/variable costs to operate business 8. Legal, accounting, insurance, utilities, ... 9. Others: travel, supplies, entertainment, ... Total $ Needs ⟶		
Later Stages of Growth 1. Increasing working capital needs 2. Building the organization 3. Increasing sales and marketing budget 4. Space 5. Inventory 6. Infrastructure: computers, phones, systems 7. All fixed/variable costs to operate business 8. Legal, accounting, insurance, utilities, ... 9. Others: travel, supplies, entertainment, ... Total $ Needs ⟶		

variable costs. You are continuing to build your organization, enhance infrastructure, accelerate your marketing and sales campaign, and develop sources of supply for inventory. Your fixation is on capturing customers, delivering products and services, and reaching breakeven sales. Beyond breakeven, your financial needs escalate further as you gain confidence in your Money Machine.

Suggestion: Pause here. Mark this page and fill in the blank columns of Exhibit 17.1. You want to answer two questions: how much money do you need at each phase, and how will you use the funds? Approximations are fine at this point. This data will be of immense value to you as you communicate with likely capital providers.

SELECT APPROPRIATE SOURCES OF CAPITAL

There are four broad categories of sources of capital: debt, equity, miscellaneous sources, and guerrilla financing (Exhibit 17.2).[1]

Debt

It will be time well spent to go to a few banks and meet with loan officers. *Make sure to bring your executive summary and financial statements with you.* This will give you an opportunity to learn firsthand how banks lend and to select the bank of your choice for a long-term relationship. You will hear that banks lend money based on solid collateral and on your ability to repay the loan. Collateral is an asset that can be sold to cover the debt in case you default on the loan. Banks do not want to own the collateral (real estate, inventory, machinery, equipment, liquid securities, accounts receivable). They simply need guarantees that your loan will be repaid according to the terms of the loan. And they will not lend money without collateral. The good news is that you will not be required to give up equity in your company under traditional lending conditions. If you have little or no collateral for a standard bank loan, you may be eligible for a loan backed by the Small Business Administration (SBA). The federal government has established a program to guarantee loans to small and emerging businesses through the SBA. A visit to their offices in your area will also be productive (www.SBA.gov). In addition to banks, you might also find family, friends, and private lenders willing to loan money for your venture, with or without collateral.

Downloadable Exhibit 17.2   Sources of Capital and Their Requirements*

Sources of Money	What Is Required
Debt (Loans) Banks Private lenders Family, friends, acquaintances Small Business Administration	Lenders want to ensure that they are paid back with appropriate interest for the risk they are taking. Lenders require collateral to guarantee your payment. Collateral is an asset that can be sold to cover debt in case of default.
Equity (Stock) Friends, family, acquaintances Working partners Private investors: Opportunistic Angels Private investors: Professional Angels Venture capitalists	Investors want to own a portion of your company so that they are rewarded generously if and when it succeeds and when there is an exit, harvest, merger, acquisition or cash-out.
Miscellaneous Sources	
Personal savings, credit cards, sale of personal assets, second job, and so on.	Brainstorm with friends and advisors. Refer to example in Chapter 3.
Leasing companies	Regular payments on equipment lease.
Factoring companies	A percentage of receivables.
Royalty lenders	A percentage of sales.
Combinations: debt and equity (warrants/options)	Creative combinations that may be attractive to certain investors.
Finance companies	Regular payments on the payback.
Third-party signature	The investor guarantees your loan for negotiated compensation (e.g., warrants).
Franchising	Franchisees pay you for the right to sell your product or service in their territory.
Stakeholder funding	Certain stakeholders may want to invest or loan (landlord, suppliers, your lawyer, etc.).
Guerrilla financing To whose advantage is it to provide money, services, or noncash exchanges? This is a powerful approach, limited only by your imagination.	Guerrilla financing is the use of your unbridled imagination. Whatever results in a mutually beneficial relationship based on nontraditional financing or noncash exchanges of goods and services.

Source: www.CompetitiveSuccess.com, "Sources of Capital and Their Requirements." Copyright © 2000 by Michael E. Gordon. Used with permission. *A blank version of this page can be downloaded from www.trumpuniversity.com/entrepreneurship101 for your personal use.*

Equity

The term *equity* is used to describe money that is provided to a business in exchange for ownership in the company. An equity investor will buy stock primarily for large potential future gains on the sale of your company. As partial owners, equity investors are your business partners. Investors may be friends, working partners, opportunistic or professional private investors ("angels"), venture capitalists, or a capital provider who might want the contractual right to buy stock in your company at a future time (stock options or warrants).

Angel and Venture Capitalist Investors

An angel investor is an individual having the money and the willingness to invest early in the life of an attractive venture for ownership of your company's stock. Similar circumstances apply to professional venture capital firms; their goal is to invest in high-potential ventures, preferably ones that are already well on their way to very rapid growth. Exhibit 17.3 will give you an understanding of what is important to these equity investors and what you can do to improve your funding success. Recall that angels and venture capitalists are rewarded only if and when your business succeeds, and if and when there is a sale, merger, or acquisition of your company. Their goal is to make significant returns on their investment (a multiple of 5 to 10 times) in the 5- to 7-year time frame.

Miscellaneous Sources

There are many sources of capital other than traditional lenders and equity investors. Here are some of the most common categories:

- Leasing companies finance certain equipment for a monthly lease repayment.
- Factoring companies provide money based on your accounts receivable.
- Royalty lenders provide money in return for a percentage of your sales.
- Finance companies may provide money on certain assets, as if they were a lease.
- Third parties may provide the bank with collateral on *your* loan, for a consideration—stock, warrants, royalties, or dividends.

Downloadable Exhibit 17.3   Improve Your Chances of Equity Investor Funding*

	What Is Important to Smart Equity Investors?	What Can You Do to Improve Funding Success?
1.	Their belief that you, the founding entrepreneur, will actually start and grow this profitable venture.	The further along the path to getting customers you are, the more interested investors will be. Capturing actual paying customers will validate your assumptions of market need, pricing, and strength of your product or service. Prepare a professional executive summary and practice making presentations to your banker, SBA's SCORE, and other knowledgeable professionals. Learn from each; improve your presentation.
2.	Your business opportunity, which is timely, compelling, unique, easy to understand, and can make money for them.	Screen your opportunity thoughtfully, according to Chapter 6. An opportunity for investors has the potential of turning into a sizable *positive Money Machine* and has the probability of generating attractive returns on their investment. The closer you are to cash flow breakeven, the more interested they will be to invest in your company.
3.	A strong, motivated, skilled team that works well together.	Savvy investors look closely at your management team. You cannot build a first-rate venture with a second-rate team. Build a team that has past successes and is mature, knowledgeable, experienced, highly committed, motivated, entrepreneurial, and headed by a CEO with a strong vision and the ability to execute.
4.	Sustainability and competitive strength.	Build competitive advantages, barriers to competitor entry, technical and proprietary know-how, differentiation, rapid customer acceptance, and market penetration (Chapter 12).
5.	Use of funds.	Give investors a clear description of how you will use their money. They want their money to stimulate growth through market penetration, new product development, and working capital. They don't want to pay for past debt, big salaries, perks, company cars, or fancy office space.
6.	A compelling executive summary and business plan.	Present the complete picture in a convincing way, without hype or salesmanship. Define why this is an opportunity for investors to participate. State your financial assumptions clearly. The financial projections must be believable.
7.	Minimum risk of loss.	Develop a chart of all the risks that might befall your company. In the second column, define your plan to eliminate, minimize, or handle each potential problem.

- Certain stakeholders may want to invest or loan—landlord, suppliers, customers, others.
- You can sell franchises if your venture is far enough along to have products, services, or business methodologies that can be cloned.

Guerrilla Financing

Guerrilla financing[2] is a state of mind rather than a discrete funding category. You have probably heard the term and even used the concepts already. The idea is to use every bit of your imagination, creativity, out-of-the-box thinking, and inventiveness to figure out unique ways to raise and conserve money. When conventional sources don't fit into your funding plan, go the nontraditional route. Bootstrapping (Chapter 7), brainstorming, and guerrilla tactics work hand in hand. They combine to enable you to move forward and to prevent you from getting stopped, even when your capital resources are limited. As you scan the list of your needs that would ordinarily cost money, figure out how to get what you want nontraditionally, and/or for the least cost. At the same time, you might uncover nontraditional investors as well. Guerrillas and bootstrappers will look anywhere and everywhere for financing. Here is a starter list:

- *Rent:* Your landlord may be willing to invest in exchange for rent.
- *Equipment:* Lease used equipment or buy at auction or on eBay.
- *Salaries:* Offer stock or future bonuses for lower wages.
- *Marketing:* Several companies can share costs in a cooperative advertising project.
- *Labor:* Use contract labor and interns. If the project is exciting, interns may join you short term, for no pay.
- *Legal services:* Your lawyer might have an interest in taking stock in your company for services.
- *Inventory:* Your suppliers might trade materials for stock in your company.
- *Using other people's credit:* They would be compensated for providing the collateral for your loan.
- *Advance payments from customers:* Ask for prepayments for future delivery.
- *Barter:* Trade goods or services for anything and everything without the exchange of money.
- *Use your unbridled imagination.*

Putting All the Sources Together

The sources of capital we have discussed are compiled in Exhibit 17.2, along with the requirements for each source.

As you look over the list of capital sources, ask yourself which are most suitable for your venture, based on your funding goal statement. At this point you are halfway through your funding plan. Your next step is to improve your chances of getting funded.

IMPROVE YOUR CHANCES OF EQUITY INVESTOR FUNDING

By way of summary, you know that banks will lend money only against collateral. You know that the miscellaneous sources have their specific requirements for providing money. You used your imagination to dredge up guerrilla financiers. That leaves equity investors. Understanding their mind-set will improve your chances of attracting equity financing. Exhibit 17.3 summarizes seven issues of importance to equity investors.

Your take-away from Exhibit 17.3 is that your deal must have home run potential to angels and venture capitalists. Why else would they invest in a risky deal and take a minority position in a privately held company? By way of example, let's assume there is an angel investor who is interested in your venture. He is considering making an investment of $100,000 and has placed a valuation of $400,000 on the worth of your business *before* his investment. After he puts money into your business, the company's total value will be $500,000, and he will own 20 percent of your company ($100,000/$500,000).

After much analysis, he projects (and prays) that your business will be sold to a strategic buyer for $2 million in five years. As a 20 percent owner, the angel would be entitled to $400,000. So what is the angel's projected return on his investment?

$$\frac{\text{Return on}}{\text{investment (ROI)\%}} = \frac{\text{Future value (FV)} - \text{Present value (PV)}}{\text{Present value}} \times 100$$

$$\text{ROI (\%)} = \frac{400,000 - 100,000}{100,000} \times 100 = 300\%$$

The equity investor did well; a 300 percent return sounds quite attractive. Now, factor in taxes and inflation. Factor in the likelihood that only 20 percent of the investor's portfolio companies will result in significant pay-offs. The other 80 percent will either die or live a small life, with no pay-off. Equity investing is risky business.

TAKE THE MOST LIKELY PATH TO EARLY-STAGE FUNDING

Let's step back and take an inventory: You have an opportunity. After studying the industry and your competition, you have designed your Money Machine and have developed an astute strategy to capture customers. Most important, you have developed financial projections for start-up and growth and have created your executive summary. With your funding plan well under development, you are positioned to raise money. Now what?

A very key decision is whether you will take equity partners. If you choose the No Equity Partners route, you will steer clear of all types of equity investors listed in Exhibit 17.2. This will eliminate partnerships with other members of your start-up team, with private investors (angels), and with any investor or lender that may want options or warrants to buy stock in your company in the future. My partner and I chose to go into business together as equity partners, and from then on we chose the No (Further) Equity Partners route for several reasons:

- We had a strong belief in our opportunity and wanted to be rewarded when the business grew.
- We wanted to keep control of all the ownership so there would be no other voices in decision making.
- We believed we could grow our business without equity investors; we reserved the possibility of bringing investors in at a later time, if needed.
- Without other owners, we could take appropriate salaries, bonuses, benefits, cars, insurance, profit sharing, and other perks.

We financed our company with personal funds, by bootstrapping, by taking it one manageable step at a time, by not trying to compress time, through bank borrowing, through equipment financing, and through very high profit margins. When we sold our company, we owned 100 percent of the equity.

The Yes Equity Partners decision leads to the consideration of *all* funding sources, shown in Exhibit 17.2.

There is not just one fixed path or process to getting funded. A typical scenario is that the founding entrepreneur will first provide money from his or her personal assets and credit cards until it gets painful. If there are other team members, often they will want to contribute money to the start-up for a slice of the ownership. Additional start-up capital can come from many sources (refer to the brainstorming exercise in Chapter 3). Some likely sources of early-stage funding are tabulated in Exhibit 17.4.

Think carefully about the advantages and consequences of each source. For example, if you take investments from family members and friends, you can imagine that at every family gathering or party, your partners will want to know how their investment is doing. "And by the way, isn't that a new car you just bought, my dear nephew (with undeclared dividends that I should be sharing)?" "And how was your family vacation to Aruba (on *our* company's money, my dear ex-friend)?"

Exhibit 17.4 Early-Stage Funding Sources

You and Your Team	Family	Friends/Angels
Personal savings	Parents	Close friends
Personal credit cards	Siblings	Not too close friends
Personal loans	Uncles/aunts	Friends of friends
Sell possessions	Spouse	Rich/poor friends
Cash in insurance policies	Children	Clueless/forgiving friends
Working partners	Close cousins	Opportunistic angels
Moonlight (second job)	Distant cousins	Professional angels
Bootstrapping		
Guerrilla financing		
SBA-backed loans		

Source: www.CompetitiveSuccess.com, "Early-Stage Funding Sources." Copyright © 2000 by Michael E. Gordon. Used with permission.

After start-up, financial needs begin to accelerate, and entrepreneurs typically seek professional lenders and equity providers. A word of advice: The longer you can stay in a frugal, penny-pinching mode to conserve cash and equity, the better off you will be in the future, as long as your growth rate is not harmed because of cash starvation. Think bootstrapping and guerrilla financing.

ORCHESTRATE THE FUNDING PROCESS

The funding process occurs in three phases. It is important to target the right sources of capital; otherwise, your precious time will be wasted.

Phase 1: Before the Meeting

This is the preparation stage. Develop a list of likely funding targets. Make contact with the individual or the organization and request a meeting. If you can find a respected third person who can introduce you, the doors will open wide. Send a compelling cover letter (without hype) along with your executive summary. Make sure you have done your homework on the funding sources: types of companies in which they invest, funding amount for a typical investment, industry preferences, success rate, and so on. Prepare for a 15- to 20-minute PowerPoint presentation, and bring back-up material in case there is strong interest. Rehearse your presentation thoroughly; role-play the meeting with an advisor.

Phase 2: During the Meeting

Leave all emotions at the door—except for passion. Communicate your venture proposition with confidence. Your basic approach should be that your company is positioned for exciting growth, that you are stable and not desperate for capital, and that a capital infusion at this time would enable the implementation of more rapid growth. Avoid exaggeration, defensiveness, and salesmanship. When you prepared your executive summary, you learned what turns investors on (Chapter 15); these are the buttons to push during the meeting. Make sure that you can justify your assumptions and financial projections. Return on investment is where the action is. This is the time to discuss your financial needs and how you will use the money. It is not the time for discussions on valuation. If it comes up during the meeting, indicate that your mind is open. During the meeting, learn about their investment selection criteria.

Phase 3: After the Meeting

It is important that your expectations be reality based. Don't expect a check writer to beat a path to you right after your presentation. After one week, it is appropriate to contact the investor to sense his or her level of interest. If there is no interest, ask for advice to improve your venture proposition and presentation. Don't be disheartened. Remember that funding is a continuing, evolutionary process. Having gone through the presentation, you are better prepared to approach new investors with confidence. Remember that keeping your company funded will be challenging and time-consuming. Your odds improve as you:

- Become obsessive-compulsive about cash flow.
- Become an expert communicator and win-win negotiator.
- Adapt, evolve, never give up.

WHAT IF THERE IS INTEREST FROM AN EQUITY INVESTOR?!!

If you are talking to a potential equity investor who is not particularly knowledgeable about the process of investing in early-stage private companies, he or she may have enough information based on your executive summary and your presentation. This could be true of your parents, relatives, friends, and some inexperienced private angel investors. A more sophisticated potential investor will ask for a full business plan (see outline in Chapter 15). If he or she is still interested, a longer second meeting will be scheduled. Shortly thereafter, he or she might begin to discuss terms and conditions of investment (term sheet). Don't begin to negotiate. This is the point to seek professional legal advice. If everything looks like a go, and a term sheet is signed, the professional investor will go through the process of due diligence.[3] During this process, all of the key issues of your business are SCRUTINIZED under a high-power magnifier to verify the assumptions, facts, and projections in your business plan. Depending on the particular investor, this can take weeks or even months.

A word of caution: In one of my investments, there was another angel who owned a very significant percentage of the company. The problem was that this investor called the CEO every day to find out how his investment was doing. He became a time-consuming nuisance, draining the CEO's time and energy. The message here is that when you are ready to take money, do your own homework on the potential investor. Due diligence is a two-way street. Ask for several other references from CEOs of your angel's other investments. If he or she doesn't have any, spell out the relationship in the form of a written memorandum: what he or she can and cannot do. In fact, write it into the term sheet.

Summary

In this chapter, you have learned to:

- Clarify your business goals.
- Understand your money needs at each stage of growth.
- Select appropriate sources of capital.
- Improve your chances of equity investor interest.
- Take the most likely path to early-stage funding.
- Orchestrate the funding process.

Getting funded is a labyrinthine process. The more you understand it, the easier it is to navigate the funding maze. The more attractive your venture, the easier it is to get funded.

Actions

The four most important actions from this chapter are to:

√ Create an astute funding plan.
√ Rehearse your PowerPoint presentation thoroughly before each investor meeting.
√ Improve your presentation after each meeting.
√ Never, ever give up! Remember, you are unstoppable. You will achieve your goals!

18

FIXATE ON

THE CUSTOMER

Albert Einstein believed that a "Theory of Everything" in physics unified the four primal forces of nature: gravity, strong nuclear force, weak nuclear force, and electromagnetic force. Our unifying theory for sustainable success in business is so much simpler:

The customer is everything!

In this chapter, we examine the customer from several perspectives:

- The importance of building a customer-centered company
- Tales of customer neglect and customer care
- Mutually beneficial customer relationships
- The welcome cost of customer capture
- Eight steps to building a customer-driven company

THE IMPORTANCE OF BUILDING A CUSTOMER-CENTERED COMPANY

It is not possible to overemphasize the importance of building a customer-centered company,[1] but I will try. By customer, I am referring not to one individual customer, but to all customers for your products or services in your marketplace.

There is no such thing as a business without willing buyers. Can there be a sustainable, profitable business that does not focus, obsess, concentrate, fixate, zero in on the customer? Most certainly not! This understanding must shape *all* of your thinking and actions as you build your business. If you rivet your attention on customer satisfaction, success will likely follow. Likely, but without guarantees. The only thing that can be guaranteed is that your company cannot be built on customer dissatisfaction. There just aren't enough apathetic customers out there. Every customer you don't get, or that you lose, is a customer that one of your competitors gains. You know this already. As a customer, you have experienced the full range of treatment, from excellent to shabby. You will go back for more, and tell your friends, or you will never go back, and you will tell your friends.

Over the years I have been appalled by the cluelessness and anticustomer behavior of some CEOs, managers, and employees. Regrettably, I am not without fault in this area. I admit to having perpetrated clueless behavior toward customers in my own businesses. If only life had an "edit undo" function to allow us to revisit and correct our mistakes. There is no such magic button. The best I can do is go into customer-recovery mode and plan how I can do better with the next customer. The issue here is not only my particular interaction with one customer. If I am running an organization with one other person, with 10, 100, or even 1,000 employees, I must create a companywide culture that is customer loving in the extreme. As leader, founder, and CEO, you must create—through leadership and training—a customer-centric culture for the perpetual satisfaction of your customer. The following two stories highlight the point.

Seeds of Discontent: A Tale of Customer Neglect

I called a garden supply catalogue company to purchase some seeds for my teaching. I use these bush beans as a metaphor for the stages of growth that all companies live through: existence, survival, success, takeoff, and maturity. At the beginning of my "Living the Entrepreneurial Experience" course, I would pass out a packet of 10 seeds to each student, with no planting instructions. These seeds represented 10 business ideas, most of which would not grow to become healthy plants. At the end of the semester, students would bring their "companies" to class to see who won the competition by growing the most productive bush. This is quite an exhilarating exercise.

I ordered the seeds and was told by the customer service rep that delivery would take 7 to 10 days. No problem; the first day of class was four weeks away. After two weeks, I called again, to check on the order, which had not arrived as promised. The customer service person said that everything was okay and on track. A week later, still not having received the seeds, I made my *third* call and explained the seeds' importance to me. The response was the same, "Don't worry, sir," and the call ended in my increased frustration. With four days remaining until the beginning of the semester, I called once again. This time, I asked for the vice president of customer service (vice president of customer disservice would have been more accurate). I insisted that a new shipment be sent out immediately by overnight carrier for early morning delivery. His reply: "We will try, sir." "I can't accept that," I retorted. "I want your personal guarantee that you will oversee the package going out the door tonight, to arrive tomorrow morning, first thing." His reply: "Sir, I can only give it my best effort."

What else was there for me to do? Then, from the other end came the unkindest cut of all: "Sir, we will have to charge you an expedited shipping fee." You can probably imagine the dark thoughts that crossed my mind at that point. But I suppressed them. "That will be fine," I said. I would not waste more time telling him how frustrated I was with his customer disservice. I received the seeds the next morning, and the semester started off successfully. But that company will never hear from me again. By the way, the first package never arrived.

You surely have your own stories about being abused, mistreated, or neglected as a customer. The airline that bumped you even though you had a ticket in hand: "Sorry about that." The seafood restaurant that served really putrid fish, along with poor service. The copy center that made excuses every time your order was bungled. The manufacturer that tried to weasel out of its warranty after its product failed. The auto rental firm that took your reservation but didn't have a car when you arrived: "Sorry about that." And on and on. On the other hand, there are enlightened CEOs, founders, and leaders who both understand the importance of creating a customer-loving culture *and who follow through*. Here is an example from my own experiences.

Midnight Marauders: A Tale of Customer Care

One afternoon, I received an urgent call from a very irate customer. The antistatic floor finish our company had sold him apparently was performing poorly. The coating had been applied the night before. But this morning, the floor was slippery and its static protection performance was inadequate. He had to shut down his manufacturing operation because of this problem. In desperation, he scheduled the floor maintenance crew to come back in after midnight to strip the poor coating and reapply a new one, not knowing whether the reapplication would work.

As CEO, I made it my personal responsibility to ensure his satisfaction. I cancelled my appointments for the rest of the day and evening. The shipping room loaded my van with 100 gallons of product from a different manufacturing lot, and I drove to his facility at midnight to work with the floor maintenance crew. By 5 A.M. the floor treatment was completed and was functioning properly. There was no slipperiness, and static protection was within specifications.

A little detective work cleared up the cause of the problem. The customer's floor maintenance crew had not followed our application instructions. They diluted the solution improperly, and then used a static-generating topcoat of their own. Both production lots of our product had actually functioned properly.

My customer was delighted that his supplier's CEO would respond personally and immediately and work through the night to solve his problem. I offered to replace the previous order at no charge, even though it was not out of specification. He would not accept my offer. I went a step further; I scheduled to have our product development specialist train his floor maintenance people until they really understood the procedure. The next day I asked for a redesign of our labels to more clearly and boldly spell out the correct application procedures. The irate customer was converted to a real supporter of our company and began to buy most of his static-control products from us. Ultimately, he became our biggest account.

The problem he experienced gave our company an opportunity to stand taller. More significant, this episode communicated an important message to everyone in our company. Everyone understood the lengths that their CEO would go to ensure unwavering customer satisfaction. My partner set the same type of example. That's how we built our customer-centric company: We walked the talk! As the leader of your company, you must do the same: Set the highest standards for customer care.

MUTUALLY BENEFICIAL CUSTOMER RELATIONSHIPS

The Customer's Perspective

Every customer makes decisions regarding which supplier to choose. She might have a vendor qualification and approval system as part of a sophisticated purchasing process with detailed specifications, or she might make decisions based on more casual guidelines, relationships, and gut feeling. In any case, her buying decisions will be based on the importance of particular criteria. In making her buying decisions, she will rate each potential supplier on a scale of worst to best (Exhibit 18.1).

The point is that your product or service must perform the needed function and meet the customer's requirements. Beyond that, other factors become important. Her decision will not be based on just one parameter—price, for example. There may be one or two key criteria that would really

Exhibit 18.1   Factors in Customers' Buying Decision

Criteria	Worst				Best
Features and benefits needed	1	2	3	4	5
Other features and benefits wanted	1	2	3	4	5
Pricing and volume discounts	1	2	3	4	5
Value for price	1	2	3	4	5
Availability; time to produce/deliver	1	2	3	4	5
After-service care	1	2	3	4	5
Reputation, integrity, and reliability	1	2	3	4	5
Supplier knowledge of customer needs	1	2	3	4	5
Commitment to satisfaction	1	2	3	4	5
Relationship with the supplier	1	2	3	4	5
Risk to customer for bad selection	1	2	3	4	5
Risk to customer in worst case	1	2	3	4	5
Unambiguous guarantees	1	2	3	4	5
Other factors?	1	2	3	4	5

Source: www.CompetitiveSuccess.com, "Factors in Customers' Buying Decision." Copyright © 2000 by Michael E. Gordon. Used with permission.

sway her decision, all other things being equal. This is what you need to know about your potential customer.

In the early stages, my company lacked a clear understanding of this multifactor analysis, and our sales force would often attempt to close a sale on the basis of price alone, thereby cutting our profit. I now realize that it was my responsibility as CEO to establish clear guidelines for our customer relationships. Obviously, your company strives to be the preferred supplier, and the more you know about your customer's purchasing requirements, the better able you are to capture that customer. Turn this concept into an action plan. Don't let it hang here as "nice to know." The most straightforward approach may simply be to ask your customer on what he will base his purchasing decision, what is most important to him, and how can you become the preferred supplier? This is the bedrock of strong customer relationships.

Your Perspective

There is another side to the equation, however. Can anyone become your customer, or should you, too, use a graded list of selection criteria? After all, some customers are unprofitable to serve. Many of these dissipate your time, taking it away from customers who represent the bread and butter of your business. This is an important point. Thoughtful choices on your part are needed; you must know who you should serve. Those choices should focus both your sales efforts *and* product/service line development. Ideal customers for our static-control company were repeat customers in global, multidivisional electronic manufacturing companies. Once we penetrated one of these accounts, we would be on the approved vendor list. That meant that orders would continue to pour in without the intense front-end spadework needed to open the new accounts. Consequently, we focused our research and development on antistatic solutions, floor finish, wrist straps, foot grounding devices, packaging materials: consumable products that needed continuous replacement.

Who do you want as customers, and what products and services do you want to offer these customers? Here is a starter list to help you to define your ideal target customer and customer base:

- Who is your primary ideal customer?
- How many customers are in your geographic market?
- What size is your most desirable target business customer: small, medium, large, Fortune 500?

- How will you handle customers with particular buying characteristics?
- How will you handle customers in different geographic areas—local, regional, national, global, virtual?
- Will you have customers willing to pay more for differentiated features or customized services?
- Will you have customers willing to pay only for the bare bones?
- Will you have repeat customers, or one-time buyers?
- How will you find customers who can lead you to new products or services?
- How will you find customers who can open doors to more business?
- Will your customers be willing to pay on time without hassle?
- Others?

Customer-company interaction is a two-way street. You want to do everything in your power to develop strong customer relationships, but only with the *right* customers. The right customers are the ones that meet your requirements on this list. If you lose sight of that principle, bizarre things can happen. For example, before we understood this "right customer" idea, our static-control company was so customer-centric that salespeople and distributors would send any and all weird orders our way. One day, I noticed a very nonstandard product being packaged for shipment. It was a static-dissipative horse blanket. We were in the business of providing products for the microelectronics industry, not horses! In my zeal to develop a customer-centric company, I lost sight of the need to develop the list of desirable customers and industries and to train our sales force accordingly. We lost money on that sale, but the good news is that at least one horse is running around without static electricity.

Suggestion: Pause here, mark this page. Take the time to specify your primary ideal customer, and the mutually beneficial company-customer relationship you must develop.

THE WELCOME COST OF CUSTOMER CAPTURE

There is always a cost to capture customers, and this should be paid willingly, gratefully, thankfully—but only if it is the right customer. In Chapter 13, where you developed your income statement, there is a line item under Total Operating Costs for Marketing and Sales. This means that you are budgeting to spend money to capture customers. For illustration, assume that you have developed a unique sporting product, to be sold through any of the following business-to-consumer mechanisms: (1) the Internet, (2) mail order, (3) retail stores, (4) direct sales, (5) telesales, (6) the Shopping Channel, (7) multilevel marketing, (8) others. Assume also that you have budgeted $25,000 for sales and marketing in the first year of operation; that your financial projection is to reach $100,000 in new sales within the first 12 months of operation; and that the average sale to one retail customer is $200.

Cost to Capture Customers

Total projected new revenue	$100,000
Total number of customers	500
Average sale per customer	$200
Sales/marketing budget	$25,000
Cost to capture average customer	$50
Cost to capture each $1 in revenue	$0.25

The point of this exercise is to highlight the fact that there is always a cost to acquiring a customer. Use your sales/marketing allocation efficiently, but do note that you are actually buying customers. When you first design your product or service, consider the customer acquisition costs very carefully, especially if there are to be no repeat sales. Based on the assumptions in this example, you will always pay $50 for each $200 customer. Is it worth $50 per order to capture one customer? If it is *the right customer*, if it fits with your market penetration strategy, and if your gross profit margins can tolerate this cost of sales, the answer is yes. If not, go back to Chapter 9 on business design options.

EIGHT STEPS TO BUILDING A CUSTOMER-CENTRIC COMPANY

A customer-centric culture does not just happen. It requires your commitment to the following eight-step program:

1. *Set your vision.* Everything starts with your view of the customer-company relationship. I am not referring to a warm and fuzzy statement that you may make on occasion. I am referring to a written credo that will set the future course of your company's

customer-centric attitudes and behaviors. Your vision statement must define in specific terms how your customers are to be treated by every member of your company.

2. *Establish a system* to quantitatively monitor customer complaints, analyze credits for return of products, and perform customer satisfaction surveys.

3. *Solicit Ideas for improvement* through brainstorming sessions, suggestion contests, and by observing the best practices of exemplary companies. Involve the entire company in the dialogue of customer-centricity. And don't forget to ask customers for ideas.

4. *Communicate continuously* at all levels of your company. This is how the mantra becomes embedded into the company's DNA. Don't take it for granted that your organization knows and understands the priority you place on the customer relationship. Teach all of your sales mechanisms how to accomplish your vision by developing the script for customer interactions. Run role-playing situations for practice. Don't leave anything to chance.

5. *Make progress visible.* How is the company doing in its customer interactions? One of America's top office furniture makers made a practice of posting a weekly scorecard of orders shipped complete and on time where people couldn't help but see it. Its vice president of operations would periodically ask a worker, "Do you know this week's score?" If the worker gave the correct answer, he or she got a crisp $100 bill on the spot!

6. *Reward exceptional customer treatment.* There is nothing so exhilarating as being honored in front of your colleagues and teammates. This reward system can be built into the employee job description and performance rating in the form of initiatives. As an example of a performance initiative, the CEO of a midsize book publisher in Illinois had a practice of giving employees a choice of $100 or half a day off whenever a customer told the CEO of their good work. By broadcasting this success, it becomes an initiative for all other employees.

7. *Set the example.* The culture of your company will respond wholeheartedly to your customer-centric behavior. A significant portion of your time should be spent with customers.

8. *Don't settle for less than you envision.* Monitor progress continuously and take appropriate action. Communicate and give feedback to any employee that will not get with the program. As a last resort, eliminate obstinate employees. There is no room in your company for people who fail to give customers their due.

SUMMARY

This chapter underscores the overarching importance of the customer to your success, but only if it is the *right* customer. The nature of the customer-company relationship needs to be mutually beneficial. It is your responsibility and challenge to build customer-centricity into the DNA of your culture. Customers cost money to capture and to maintain. Welcome these costs as a means of building strong customer relationships. The chapter closes with an eight-step program to accomplish your vision.

Actions

√ Make a commitment to building a customer-centered company. Create a credo for your vision.

√ Develop clear guidelines as to who is and is not your customer. Communicate these guidelines to all of your selling mechanisms.

√ Embed the eight steps to building a customer-loving company into your company culture.

19

LAUNCH YOUR VENTURE!

We have come a long way: nineteen chapters, many case examples, frameworks, visual metaphors, concepts, and war stories from Donald Trump and the Trump Organization. And now for this penultimate and most exhilarating action: launching your venture!

What's wrong with Figure 19.1? We think of the start-up of a business as an ignition, an event, a discrete moment in time when there is liftoff. But the word "launch" is inappropriate. It doesn't happen this way. What *does* happen is a first small, seemingly insignificant step, followed by other small steps. Step by small step, your venture begins to *coalesce* and move forward on its journey.

It is not dramatic to think of the start of your business as a coalescence, but in fact this is precisely what it is. And you have already started to live the entrepreneurial process. By studying and taking action on the previous 18 chapters, you have selected an attractive opportunity; studied your competition and the industry dynamics; considered how you are going to make money; devised an astute strategy; developed financial projections; learned about bootstrapping, raising money, and negotiation; begun to focus on the customer; and captured your vision in the form of your executive summary. From my perspective, you have already coalesced your business. You now need to accomplish the next six small steps to coalesce even further:

Figure 19.1   Launch Your Venture

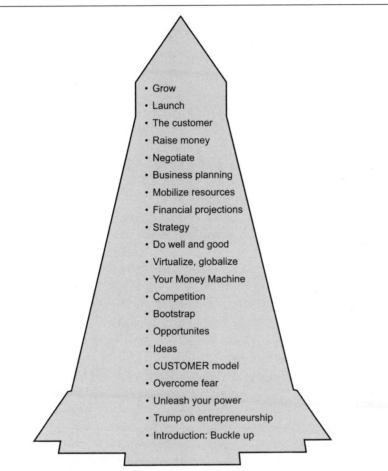

- Grow
- Launch
- The customer
- Raise money
- Negotiate
- Business planning
- Mobilize resources
- Financial projections
- Strategy
- Do well and good
- Virtualize, globalize
- Your Money Machine
- Competition
- Bootstrap
- Opportunites
- Ideas
- CUSTOMER model
- Overcome fear
- Unleash your power
- Trump on entrepreneurship
- Introduction: Buckle up

Source: www.CompetitiveSuccess.com, "Launch Your Venture." Copyright © 2006 by Michael E. Gordon. Used with permission.

Step 1: Create your business identity.

Step 2: Mobilize resources.

Step 3: Develop milestone charts.

Step 4: Take action on your To-Do Lists.

Step 5: Understand your keys to success and critical risks.

Step 6: Capture the first magic customer.

I will illustrate these six steps using examples from three of my start-ups: AngelDeals.com, Venture-Preneurs Network, and Plastic Systems, Inc.

STEP 1: CREATE YOUR BUSINESS IDENTITY

AngelDeals.com is a virtual business whose mission it is to assist in getting entrepreneurs funded over the Web. To create my business identity, I went to the site www.Register.com to find a domain name for my venture. Because the goal of my network was to connect entrepreneurs with private angel investors, I registered the name AngelDeals.com. I then went to City Hall in Boston and paid $50 for a business certificate permitting me to do business in Boston for four years under the name of AngelDeals.com. This is called a DBA, "doing business as." At a later stage, I would form the company properly, as a Chapter C corporation, a Sub Chapter S corporation, an LLC, or a nonprofit 501(C)(3) organization through a business lawyer. (If you are very limited in resources, you can go to the library and find books on how to form your own corporation; alternatively, use the Internet: http://smallbusiness.findlaw.com/business-structures/business-structures-quickstart.html. However, I strongly recommend that you get professional legal advice regarding the formation of your business.)

Next, I went to a local bank and opened a checking account under my name, doing business as AngelDeals.com. I deposited $500 into this free checking account and ordered free checks. (Shop around; there are banks that will bend over backward to give you free checking and checks.) I then went to a local office supply store and ordered professional-looking business cards. Finally, I created the format for letterhead and envelopes in Microsoft Word in my computer. In less than five hours, I had my identity.

Why is this important for you? The identity grows on you, and every time you hand out a business card or send a letter or e-mail or write a check, you are telling the world "Here comes my business!" And as you grow into your new identity, you become unstoppable.

STEP 2: MOBILIZE RESOURCES

The resource list for the start-up of AngelDeals.com looked like Exhibit 19.1. You will be well rewarded if you pay particular attention to mobilizing the most effective resources (Chapter 14). Without sufficient

Downloadable Exhibit 19.1   Needed Resources for the Start-Up of AngelDeals.com*

Start-Up Resources	Source/Actions	Use of Funds
Initial capital	Personal finances	Total allocated: $8,000
Web designer	www.DBGDesign.com	$2,000
Web technician	Independent contractor from staffing agency: I did not want to hire employees during the development phase.	$20 per hour
Webmaster	Outsourced: I found a talented technologist who also hosted my site.	$360 per year for hosting, plus hourly or contract rate for development
Interns from colleges	Built content on the site	Free: I had the support of many motivated and smart college interns.
Office	Home-based	Free
Infrastructure: computers, printers, software, cabling, and other	Three computer systems needed in development phase	Already owned, except for software and cables: $300
Sponsors	Prestigious firms in Boston for credibility	Non cash exchange for sponsorship initially
Advisors	Personal friends	Free
Marketing: generating traffic to the site	Alliances: other networks, mutual links	Free reciprocal link exchanges

Source: www.CompetitiveSuccess.com, "Needed Resources for the Start-Up of AngelDeals.com." Copyright © 2000 by Michael E. Gordon. Used with permission. ***A blank version of this page can be downloaded from www.trumpuniversity .com/entrepreneurship101 for your personal use.***

resources, you will not be able to accomplish the needed tasks on time and to the highest levels of achievement.

STEP 3: DEVELOP MILESTONE CHARTS

A milestone chart defines all key events that must occur to start and grow your venture. I explained how to create one of these in Chapter 14. In all of my endeavors, I have found it essential to visualize what needed to be done daily, weekly, monthly, and yearly. Figure 19.2 shows the first milestone chart for the development and start-up of AngelDeals.com.

Take particular note of the arrows. They are there so that you do not lose sight of the timing to reach your primary goal. Each milestone screams at you what to do and when to do it. If you miss one milestone, the

Figure 19.2   Milestone Chart for the Start-Up of AngelDeals.com

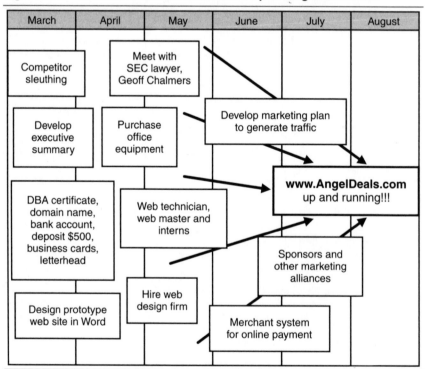

Source: www.CompetitiveSuccess.com, "Milestone Chart for the Start-Up of AngelDeals.com." Copyright © 2000 by Michael E. Gordon. Used with permission.

scream becomes a *roar*. Tape these charts on the wall over your desk. It is hard to be in denial when this chart stares back at you.

STEP 4: TAKE ACTION ON YOUR TO-DO LISTS

Milestone planning requires a companion series of daily, weekly, and monthly To-Do Lists. Each milestone by itself does not take action. Each milestone is merely one stepping stone that needs to be reached in order for you to arrive at your final destination. Your To-Do List is a tabulation of these specific tasks.

STEP 5: UNDERSTAND YOUR KEYS TO SUCCESS AND CRITICAL RISKS

The success of your venture will depend on a limited number of factors. If you pay particular attention to these few key factors, you will maximize your chance of succeeding. Critical risks are potential threats facing your venture that you may be able to anticipate and to deal with, preferably in advance.

There are several keys to the success of AngelDeals.com, but I cannot share them with you. The same goes for critical risks. The competitive landscape is such that I would be a clueless entrepreneur if I published the keys to my own success and my potential critical risks. This would be like showing the enemy my battle plan. However, I can give you the six keys to success for my face-to-face Venture-Preneurs Network, along with its critical risks:

Keys to Success for Venture-Preneurs Network

1. Each and every meeting had to deliver significant value to *all* attendees and sponsors. Otherwise, attendance would decline. Less than best does not work. The primary goal for the attendees was to connect with important door openers. All attendees had color-coded badges so that no one would waste time talking to low-priority contacts. During the meetings, my staff and I focused on bringing people together, as if we were hosting a social gathering.
2. Entrepreneurs wanted to connect only with capital providers, so we invited investors at no charge to maximize attendance.

3. Investors wanted to look at prescreened deals only, and I personally consulted for each presenting entrepreneur (fee based) to ensure that the venture looked attractive to the extent possible.
4. Each and every meeting needed buzz. I worked diligently to bring in world-class speakers.
5. My sponsors had to receive extensive visibility through introductions and presentations by their companies.
6. I was creating a personal and professional brand for myself, as well as growing my consulting company.

Critical Risks for Venture-Preneurs Network

The main risk was that other networks could copy my innovations and methods, and many did. They selected my best practices. My business methodology could not be protected. If competitors had deeper pockets, a bigger team, and a determination for dominance, they could become serious threats. My plan to deal with competition was two pronged:

1. To continuously build momentum through intense marketing, particularly through mutually-beneficial marketing alliances.
2. To deliver meetings that were of significant value to the attendees. I wanted attendees who would enthusiastically return and bring their colleagues.

STEP 6: CAPTURE THE FIRST MAGIC CUSTOMER

Now you are ready for the BIG TIME: getting your first customer! When you actually get your first customer, everyone thinks differently about you and your business. You are no longer a development-stage company; you are an early-stage operating company. You had your vision all along. You went through the tortuous multistep entrepreneurial process and it is all coming to fruition. Before that first customer, you were untried. But that one customer brings everything together. Your credibility goes sky high.

I can recall vividly the exact moment when my partner and I produced the first injection-molded part for an honest-to-goodness paying customer. We had been building our plastics factory for almost two exhilarating and frustrating years. The customer was Summagraphics. We got the job because their molder was not able to produce parts to their specifications. Words cannot describe our exuberance! We began to notice the change in our own focus. We were not starting the company anymore; we were thinking about how to fill the order and to capture more customers.

How do you capture that first paying customer? Brainstorm. Using the skills you learned in Chapter 3, bring together a group of imaginative, positive, and willing stakeholders to help you invent ways to capture the first magic customer. Here is an example of brainstormed ideas:

- Buy the customer. After all, there is always a cost to capture customers, usually in the form of marketing and advertising dollars. Pay these willingly and creatively.
- Overpay whatever is necessary (within reason).
- Give serious guarantees: money back, no ifs, ands, or buts.
- Replace with next-generation model at no charge.
- Take your potential customer out for an expensive dinner.
- Explain how important it is to have her as a first customer.
- Customize the product for him with no obligation on his part.
- Take the first order at the *most* nominal price.
- Make it worth her while in terms of price, customization, delivery, packaging.
- Suggest that his testimonial be used in an article if he is delighted with the performance of the product or service.
- Find door openers through referrals from friends, colleagues, or other contacts.
- If she places the order, use her company as a beta site—a test location.
- Offer a free trial for one month with no obligations and purchasing decision later.
- For a retail store, offer the first 100 customers 50 percent off the list price.
- Try unusual marketing techniques (guerrilla marketing).[1]
- Use your personal power—whatever you have to do to get that first customer.
- Mobilize all available resources to help you.
- Personally hand out brochures, flyers, ads on street corners.
- Use the funnel. For every 100 possible leads that go into the mouth, if 10 percent are interested, and if only one is converted to a purchase order, you have succeeded. However, if you can improve your conversion rate at each step, you are on your way to a real success.

Using this as a starter list, continue to brainstorm for your own start-up. *Your first customer will happen.* Guaranteed!

So, your start-up isn't a rocket after all. There is no blastoff. Instead, starting and growing your entrepreneurial business will be accomplished through a progressive series of steps. Each properly completed step will bring you closer to your goal: a profitable Money Machine that will keep you in the chips for many years and that, one day, you'll be able to sell to a multidivisional corporation or pass on to your children.

So take it one step at a time. Assure that each step is completed. And when you've done the last of them—and latched onto a paying customer—you will have crossed an important threshold. If you ask "Now, am I an entrepreneur?" a voice inside will shout, **"YES!"**

SUMMARY

The start-up of your venture is not an ignition. Start-up occurs through a stepwise process, a coalescence of many individual actions. Once you have identified an opportunity and created an executive summary, there are six steps that will coalesce your venture up to, and beyond zero stage:

1. Create your business identity.
2. Mobilize resources.
3. Develop milestone charts.
4. Take action on your To-Do Lists.
5. Understand your keys to success and critical risks.
6. *Capture the first magic customer!*

When you have done this, YOUR VENTURE IS LAUNCHED!

Actions

√ Give yourself a pat on the back for what you have accomplished, and a shove out the door to where the action is.
√ Success is a decision.[2] Make your decision to succeed.
√ If you have gotten to this point and have not started your business, REREAD THIS BOOK!
√ Read on to the final chapter: Suffer Growing Pains Joyfully.

20

SUFFER GROWING
PAINS JOYFULLY

Launching your business is one thing; keeping it on a healthy growth trajectory is something else. Let's look into the near future. Your venture is off the ground and you are exhilarated to be in business for yourself. Due to your relentless persistence, your ability to make good decisions, and some luck, your company is growing. You are full of confidence because you have done something important for yourself, your family, the community, your stakeholders, your employees—and for the IRS.

What will you experience as your business grows?

- The pursuit of strategic opportunities: Gordon's Value Cycle *plus* The Power of Zero
- Stages of growth—some painful; always challenging
- Your personal transition from manager to leader
- The challenges of steering your company through the disruptive global changes
- The need for continuous strategic planning

The Pursuit of Strategic Opportunities: Gordon's Value Cycle *plus* The Power of Zero

Consider this: While studying fashion design at The Art Institutes, you conceive a business opportunity for a line of audacious, cheeky clothing for the 15- to 35-year-old market. Using your creativity and sewing skills, you develop prototypes and test consumer demand by showing the clothing to many of your friends and youthful relatives. It is a WOW! Scraping together every last dollar and maxing out your credit cards, you open a retail boutique in New York City near Greenwich Village to sell and brand your own label—*NY Cheek*. To your unrestrained delight, the product line is catching on. Your creations are flying off the shelves. You project that your business will capture retail sales of $200,000 in the first year and $500,000 in the fifth year.

Enter Gordon's Value Cycle. Figure 20.1 depicts all of the critical value-adding activities that you and your company perform to convert your opportunity into a Money Machine.

Figure 20.1   Gordon's Value Cycle for *NY Cheek Before* Power of Zero

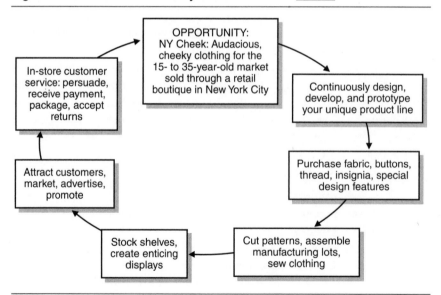

Source: www.CompetitiveSuccess.com, "Gordon's Value Cycle for NY Cheek Before Power of Zero." Copyright © 2002 by Michael E. Gordon. Used with permission.

With your OPPORTUNITY at the top of the cycle, go around clockwise and follow the sequential actions that add value for your customers—the greater the value added, the greater the profits.[1] Look closely. The only real value you add is in the first step: *creating unique designs*. Other than your own creations, what do you have?—rented space to sell other designer labels and no real competitive advantage.

Using the POWER OF ZERO (Chapter 2), you start adding zeros to the fifth-year projected sales. You ask, "How can I build this business to $5 million in five years?" You add another zero: "How can I build this business to $50 million? To $500 million?" And deep inside you, a confident but barely audible voice whispers: "you can do it!" *But how?* You need significant money, an action-oriented team, and a strategic plan. Do you build out company-owned stores, sell through global distribution, or market over the Internet or the TV buying channel? After much strategizing with advisors, you come up with several reasons why your boldest vision is to grow through global franchising:

- Rapid market penetration
- Leveraging your brand
- Maximum scalability with least risk
- Most astute method of raising capital

It is the *HOW* that is crucial. How can you accomplish such a bold vision? Figure 20.2 is a strategic reconstruction of your business based on rapid growth through global franchising.

Note that your value-added activities change radically. Your unique, audacious designs are still the essence of your brand, but now your company must build core capabilities in franchising and global marketing. The reconstructed Value Cycle defines these new activities. Here is the home-run with bases loaded: The questions in the center of the cycle lead to another Power of Zero!

- What are the keys to my company's success?
- Are there other revenue models to be exploited?
- Can my company's core capabilities be leveraged further?
- Are there global sourcing and marketing enablers?
- Where are the new opportunities?
- What are the potential vulnerabilities and threats?

The Value Cycle in conjunction with the Power of Zero is empowering to the nth degree.

Figure 20.2 Gordon's Value Cycle for *NY Cheek After* Power of Zero

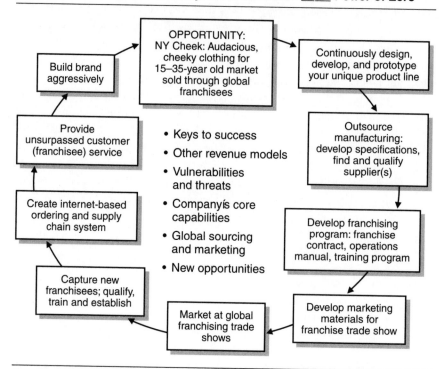

PREDICTABLE STAGES OF GROWTH

Your business, like most others, will pass through several predictable stages of growth. You and it will experience growing pains as you move from stage to stage.[2] This was my experience in our plastics company.

Stage 1: Existence

In the Existence stage, just beyond Zero stage, I was consumed with obtaining customers, delivering acceptable products and services, and having enough money to keep afloat. Staying alive was my preoccupation.

After almost two years of setting up our plastics factory, we were ready to take in our first customer. A friend put us in touch with a company in the electronics industry that provided digitizing graphic tablets and styluses. The company was having problems with its current plastics supplier, and we were given the contract. We hired a molding technician to run the factory in our absence. Cash flow was manageably negative; it wasn't a life threatening issue because my partner and I were continuing in our day jobs. Our new-born company didn't crash and burn. It was alive and functioning! And slowly it began to attract more customers.

Stage 2: Survival

Now that our company had some customers who accepted our products and services, the primary issue was survival. Questions that came to mind were: Do our products and services have sufficient profit potential? Can we achieve breakeven sales in a timely way—the sooner the better (Chapter 13)—and generate enough positive cash flow to finance growth? Or raise more money? Cash flow was now becoming an issue. The financing needs induced by growth included:

- Hiring additional employees
- Selling and marketing
- Building inventory
- Improving infrastructure
- Covering increasing overhead expenses

We joined the company full time in this Survival stage, brimming with confidence that the business had sufficient profit potential to pay our salaries and to generate adequate cash flow for growth. Decision making was a joint endeavor. Together, we engineered each new job that came in—tool and part design, material selection, molding conditions, and process control—until it could be handed over to our molding technician for production. We also reached agreement on new hires, new equipment needs, marketing and advertising expenditures.

Stage 3: Success, Profitability, and Stabilization

Growth continued into Stage 3. Our organization became more complex. We now had many employees under the supervision of functional managers: marketing and sales, operations, administration, financial management, R&D, and so forth. More of my time shifted from executing specific tasks to influencing functional managers. My preoccupations were financing growth, broadening the product offerings, increasing cash flow, hiring new talent, and building a high-performance culture.

The business was now strong and looking toward the future. At this point, other thoughts cropped up: Should we continue to grow the company, or sell it? We had created substantial value and were beginning to ponder a simpler, less stressful life. The pressures of managing a rapidly growing enterprise were both exhilarating and intense.

Stage 4: Takeoff

As in Stage 3, the issues in the takeoff stage were mobilizing and employing more resources—human, financial, physical, knowledge, infrastructure, and others. Cash flow was a significant concern at all times. Long-range strategy and sustainability become my focus. The company grew to be multidivisional. Our second business was in static control for the microelectronics industry, which overshadowed our plastics business in size and growth rate. We began to explore a third division in chemical spill control, as well as potential acquisitions in other fields.

I was continuously grappling with the personal issues of evolving from manager to leader. This was a very difficult transition for me personally, because I leaned toward micromanagement. It was during Stage 4 that we decided to sell our company if the right buyer came along. The right buyer came along. A public British company wanted us and made an attractive offer. Also, the currency ratio between the British pound and the dollar was favorable, and we sold our baby.

Stage 5: Resource Maturity

In the resource maturity stage, the company is usually quite multidivisional. Its strategy will have changed dramatically. When it was a single-industry business, its strategic focus was to gain competitive advantages and share of market by differentiating from the competition. Now, with a presence in many industries, the corporate strategy is to decide what businesses the company should be in, and how to manage the portfolio of business units. The company is similar to a mutual fund, with the difference being that it has control of the operations of each business.

Why do these predictable transitions lead to growing pains? From my personal experience, the turbulence occurred because of the layers of new managers and supervisors that came in as we grew. Not only was my job changing, but when a new layer of management was established, job descriptions and reporting relationships throughout the company had to change.

From Manager to Leader: Making the Transition

You will need to change from manager to leader as soon as possible. Like a caterpillar on the path to butterflyhood, you have no choice here. You must assume the mantle of leadership because your business demands this from you. If you can't evolve, replace yourself. In my company, I found it very challenging to evolve beyond micromanaging. In my zeal to make sure that everything was always on track, I kept myself involved in *all* aspects of the company: operations, inventory levels, production scheduling, quality control, new product development, marketing, sales, administration, budgeting, staffing, international sales, finance, customer service—everything. In fact, to control cash flow, I personally signed all purchase orders over $500 and all outgoing checks. From the perspective of hindsight, I now understand the importance of rising to the leadership position and paying attention to the 10 Leadership Actions listed below:

Ten Leadership Actions
1. Establishing the vision and mission for the company.
2. Leading change in response to opportunities and threats.
3. Developing an entrepreneurial, high-performance company culture.
4. Training the management team and line supervisors.
5. Growing profitably with a focus on sustainability.
6. Formulating and implementing an astute strategic plan.
7. Building and allocating resources.
8. Setting the moral tone of the company.
9. Managing risk.
10. Communicating continuously to all levels of the company.

NAVIGATING DISRUPTIVE GLOBAL CHANGES

We are living in an amazing period of irreversible global hypertransformation[3] that is rippling through every part of our business and personal lives. I am referring to the dynamics portrayed in Figure 5.1: Turbulent Global Changes. In his national best-selling book *The World Is Flat*, Thomas Friedman discusses "Ten Forces That Flattened the World" that are causing these rapid changes we experience every single day.[4] His 10 flattening forces are:

1. The fall of the Berlin Wall and the information revolution.
2. The emergence of the Internet browser (Netscape).
3. Work flow software.
4. Open source software.
5. Outsourcing.
6. Off-shoring (General Electric).
7. Supply-chaining (Wal-Mart).
8. Insourcing (UPS).
9. The search engines (Google.com).
10. The rapid growth of digital, wireless, mobile, and virtual technologies.

Adding fuel to these 10 factors is what Friedman calls the Triple Convergence of (1) all 10 flatteners, (2) new business methods being adopted by the new generation, and (3) more than 3 billion people in China, India, Latin America, Russia, and Eastern Europe coming into the global market economy. I have four words for all of this:

Bring on the changes!

We are entrepreneurs because we view these disruptive changes as a goldmine of potential opportunities. Disruptive change creates opportunities for the alert and ambitious. While the losers are busy moaning or defending the status quo, the winners are busily latching onto that which is new and appealing. But these disruptive changes and opportunities are two-edged swords. Your corporate well-being will require you to develop a self-preserving paranoia as you look over your shoulder for competitor thrusts and technological disruptions. Take the Polaroid Corporation as an example. I still recall the collapse of Polaroid with disbelief. I worked for this superlative company for 10 years, and it is inconceivable to me that this once vibrant, $2.3 billion company went into bankruptcy and has shrunk to little more than a brand name. The company was truly outstanding: world-class research and development, state-of-the-art optics, battery technology, engineering and manufacturing capabilities, hundreds of cutting-edge patents, pick-and-place assembly technology, precise multilayer film coating, sophisticated chemical synthesis, one of the 10 greatest brand names in the world—*the ability to accomplish anything it set its mind to.*

On the surface, the company's downfall resulted from the inability of Polaroid's leadership to adapt to disruptive technological changes as digital photography was rapidly emerging. But that oversimplifies the problem. As a Polaroid insider for a decade, I believe that this disaster could have been foreseen and avoided! How? By paying attention to my comprehensive CUSTOMER model (Chapter 4) and by using the strategic planning cycle shown in Figure 20.3.

Notice how the key elements in the cycle form the acronym AVOID. Together, they can help you avoid the business-killing impact of change and find ways of benefiting from it. Following the cycle, you begin by developing an objective assessment of internal and external forces that will affect your business. From that assessment, you—and your colleagues—develop a vision of how your business can identify and exploit new

Figure 20.3   Gordon's Strategic Planning Cycle: AVOID at Your Peril!

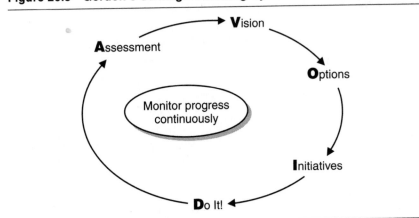

Source: www.CompetitiveSuccess.com, "Gordon's Strategic Planning Cycle: AVOID at Your Peril!" Copyright © 2000 by Michael E. Gordon. Used with permission.

opportunities created by change. You then develop a set of feasible options, turn the best of them into practical, market and financial-based initiatives, and DO IT! Even as you do it and reap success, you keep your eyes open, continually assessing the environment.

To understand the AVOID cycle more completely, put yourself in the shoes of Polaroid's CEO in 1995. Then go through each element with me.

Assessment

It is not possible to develop an astute strategy before you fully understand the external industry dynamics and the internal strengths and weaknesses of your company. This is *assessment*.

So what is going on in Polaroid's world in 1995? Externally, the obvious threat is the inevitable and rapid emergence of digital photography. Polaroid is a single-industry instant photography firm, and red flags are waving furiously in 1995 that the company is in imminent danger. Its only business unit is about to be seriously disrupted by the new technology. Internally, your R&D is world-class, but your corporate culture does not encourage the entrepreneurial. In the past, your company had demonstrated its ability to accomplish technological miracles. However, too few technological miracles have resulted in new money-making business units.

Vision

Once you have gone through the process of intelligence gathering and soul searching, you are ready to pronounce the boldest vision for the future Polaroid. You envision a world-class, worldwide, broadly diversified company, similar to, but surpassing, 3M for technological brilliance and innovation. *You are not limited to photography, imaging, or graphics.* You will be opportunistic in the pursuit of *any and all* markets that can lead to profitable diversification. You foresee a strong balance sheet, superb profit margins, and high valuation resulting from your applied technological excellence. (Sadly, this was not the vision that Polaroid had in 1995.)

Options

You have several different courses of action to accomplish your vision of rapid, broad technological diversification:

- Hire an entrepreneurial director of homegrown technologies to commercialize existing patents and know-how.
- Hire an entrepreneurial director of acquisitions for emerging technologies.
- Hire an entrepreneurial director of global diversification through acquisitions.
- Hire an entrepreneurial director of strategic global partnerships.

And the answer is . . . ALL OF THE ABOVE, and urgently!

Initiatives

Learn from the best. Absorb and implement best practices from the great companies in the world: 3M, Toyota, Procter & Gamble, General Electric, and the like. Your first initiative is to minimize cash outflow to the extreme. Your second initiative is to clean up the balance sheet by divesting all nonessential real estate, and other nonperforming assets. The company needs this cash to stay alive and to implement your vision for technological diversification. Initiative number 3 is to make sure your organization is the leanest, fastest, and *most entrepreneurial*—everyone must add value or be gone. Initiative number 4 is to commercialize every one of your core capabilities and technologies.

Do It!

Some strategies are doomed to fail because they cannot be implemented. All strategies are doomed to fail if the CEO has not built a proactive management team and company culture that can DO IT, one that is able to implement its strategic plan. As you implement, *monitor progress continuously:* Having a plan means (almost) nothing unless you have established the measurement system to ensure that people are delivering on the plan—and that means delivering superior, sustainable, financial performance, and at the same time, managing risk.

So what does the fate of the once mighty Polaroid have to do with the you, and the well-being of your own company? The AVOID principles apply to companies of all sizes—from the tiniest to the mightiest. The business landscape is littered with the wreckage of companies, large and small, that failed to change as the world around them changed. Don't become one of them. Recognize that change creates opportunities for growth and diversification. It can help you survive and thrive as others fall into decline and disappear. Chances are that some change in the external environment created the opportunity you exploited to launch your business. Stay alert to new change-induced opportunities to grow and prosper.

SUMMARY

In this chapter, we looked at the forces you will experience as your company grows:

- The pursuit of strategic opportunities: Gordon's Value Cycle *plus* The Power of Zero
- Growing pains as your business goes through predictable stages of growth
- Your personal transition from manager to leader
- The challenges of steering your company through the dramatic global changes that are occurring
- The need for continuous strategic planning

Most of all, this chapter speaks to the achievement of your entrepreneurial dream. It speaks of great courage, unbridled passion, laser focus and massive commitment. The power of commitment is this:

Until one is committed, there is hesitancy, the chance to draw back, always ineffectiveness. Concerning all acts of initiative (and creation), there is one elementary truth the ignorance of which kills countless ideas and splendid plans: that the moment one definitely commits oneself, then providence moves too. All sorts of things occur to help one that would never otherwise have occurred. A whole stream of events issue from the decision, raising in one's favour all manner of unforeseen incidents and meetings and material assistance, which no man could have dreamed would have come his way.

Whatever you can do or dream you can, begin it. Boldness has genius, power and magic in it. Begin it now.

—J. W. von Goethe

NOTES

Chapter 1: Trump on Entrepreneurship

1. George H. Ross, *Trump Strategies for Real Estate* (Hoboken, NJ: John Wiley & Sons, 2005), p. 4.

Chapter 2: Unleash Your Entrepreneurial Power

1. For further literature on entrepreneurship, the following two textbooks are recommended: Jeffrey A. Timmons and Stephen Spinelli, *New Venture Creation: Entrepreneurship for the Twenty-first Century* (New York: McGraw Hill/Irwin, 2007); and William D. Bygrave and Andrew Zacharakis, *The Portable MBA in Entrepreneurship*, 4th ed. (Hoboken, NJ: John Wiley & Sons, 2005).
2. Roger Fisher and William Ury, *Getting to Yes: Negotiating Agreement without Giving In* (Boston: Houghton Mifflin, 1981).
3. Charles H. Kepner and Benjamin B. Tregoe, *The Rational Manager: A Systematic Approach to Problem Solving and Decision Making* (Princeton, NJ: Kepner Tregoe, 1997).

Chapter 3: Feel the Fear—Do It Anyway

1. Alex F. Osborn, *Applied Imagination: Principles and Procedures of Creative Problem-Solving*, 3rd ed. (New York: Scribner's, 1993).
2. Shakti Gawain, *Creative Visualization: Use the Power of Your Imagination to Create What You Want in Your Life* (Novato, CA: New World Library, 2002).

Chapter 4: Start Right—Build on the CUSTOMER Model

1. Richard Whiteley and Diane Hessan, *Customer Centered Growth: Five Proven Strategies for Building Competitive Advantage* (New York: Addison-Wesley, 1996).
2. Larry Bossidy & Ram Charan, *Execution: The Discipline of Getting Things Done* (New York: Crown Publishing Group 2002).
3. Michael E. Gordon, *Gordon's CUSTOMER Model: Nine Factors for Competitive Success*, The Center for Competitive Success (Cambridge, MA, 2000).

Chapter 5: Scour the World for Ideas

1. Myra M. Hart et al., *Boston Duck Tours: Has Boston Gone Quackers?* case no. 9-898-189 (Boston: Harvard Business School Publishing, 1998).

Chapter 6: Select One (and Only One) Opportunity

1. Michael E. Gordon, *Case Study: Plastechnology*, The Center for Competitive Success, Cambridge, Massachusetts, 1995.
2. Discussions with Dr. Edward Marram, founder of Geo-Centers, Inc., and director of the Arthur M. Blank Center for Entrepreneurship, 2006, Babson College, Babson Park, MA.
3. Robert Blunden and Joseph N. Fry, *The Kettle Creek Canvas Company (A)* case study no. 9A87M16 (Ontario, Canada: Richard Ivey School of Business, 1985).
4. This material has been extracted from Jeffrey A. Timmons and Stephen Spinelli, *New Venture Creation*, 7th ed. (New York: McGraw-Hill/Irwin, 2007), chap. 4.

Chapter 7: Bootstrap

1. This material has been extracted from Inc. Magazine, September 21, 1992.
2. Discussions with Jack Doherty, founder and CEO of College Hype, www.collegehype.com, 2006.
3. See note 1.

Chapter 8: Plan for the War with Your Competitors

1. Michael E. Porter, *Competitive Strategy: Techniques for Analyzing Industries and Competitors* (New York: Free Press, 1998), p. 4.
2. See note 1.

3. Sun Tzu, *The Art of War*, trans. Thomas Cleary (Boston: Shambala, 1988).
4. Amarnath Bhide, *"Hustle as Strategy,"* Harvard Business Review (September 1, 1986).

Chapter 10: Virtualize and Globalize

1. Discussions with Myron Waldman, president and founder of www.neededhere.net, a web consulting, design, construction, and traffic-building firm.
2. Myron Gladwell, *The Tipping Point: How Little Things Can Make a Big Difference* (Boston: Little, Brown, 2002).
3. For further literature on web strategy, design, and traffic, the reader is referred to the following books: Robin Nobles and Susan O'Neil, *Streetwise Maximize Web Site Traffic: Build Web Site Traffic Engine Placement* (Holbrook, MA: Adams Media Corp., 2002); William Stanek, *Increase Your Web Traffic in a Weekend*, 3rd ed. (Rocklin, CA: Prima Tech, 2000).

Chapter 11: Do Well and Do Good?

1. Christine Arena, *Cause for Success: 10 Companies That Put Profit Second and Came in First* (Novato, CA: New World Library, 2004).

Chapter 12: Devise a Winning Strategy

1. For further reading on strategy, the reader is referred to the following: Michael E. Porter, *Competitive Strategy: Techniques for Analyzing Industries and Competitors* (New York: Free Press, 1998); Michael E. Porter, *Competitive Advantage: Creating and Sustaining Superior Performance* (New York: Free Press, 1998); Michael H. Morris, *Entrepreneurial Intensity: Sustainable Advantages for Individuals, Organizations, and Societies* (Westport, CT: Quorum Books, 1998); Liam Fahey and Robert M. Randall, *The Portable MBA in Strategy* (New York: John Wiley & Sons, 1994); Richard A. D'Aveni with Robert Gunther, *Hyper-Competitive Rivalries: Competing in Dynamic Environments* (New York: Free Press, 1995).
2. Michael E. Porter, *Competitive Strategy: Techniques for Analyzing Industries and Competitors* (New York: Free Press, 1998).
3. Michael E. Porter, *Competitive Advantage: Creating and Sustaining Superior Performance* (New York: Free Press, 1998).
4. "Buying Air Time: Fractional Ownership Slashes Private-Plane Costs," *Fortune Small Business* (June 2006): 106.

5. James C. Collins and Jerry I. Porras, *Built to Last: Successful Habits of Visionary Companies* (New York: HarperCollins, 2002), pp. 68–71.
6. For further reading on marketing, the reader is referred to the following: Don Sexton, *Trump University Marketing 101* (Hoboken, NJ: John Wiley & Sons, 2006); Jay Conrad Levinson, *Guerrilla Marketing: Secrets for Making Big Profits from Your Small Business* (New York: Houghton Mifflin, 1998).
7. See note 3.
8. Sheryl Overlan, Edward Marram, Glenn Kaplus, and Leslie Charm, *Patio Rooms of America (A)* (Babson Park, MA: Babson College, January 2005).
9. Joe Girard with Stanley H. Brown, *How to Sell Anything to Anybody* (New York: Simon & Schuster, 1997).

Chapter 13: Project Your Growth and Profitability

1. For further reading on financial statements, refer to the following textbooks: William D. Bygrave and Andrew Zacharakis, *The Portable MBA in Entrepreneurship*, 4th ed. (Hoboken, NJ: John Wiley & Sons, 2005), pp. 141–165; John A. Tracy, *How to Read a Financial Report* (Hoboken, NJ: John Wiley & Sons, 1994); Linda Pinson and Jerry Jinnett, *Keeping the Books: Basic Record Keeping and Accounting for the Small Business* (Chicago: Dearborn Trade Publishing, 2004); and David H. Bangs Jr., *The Cash Flow Control Guide: Methods to Understand and Control the Small Business' Number One Problem* (Denver, CO: Upstart Publishing, 1990).

Chapter 14: Mobilize Powerful Resources Quickly

1. For a general treatment of entrepreneurial resources, the reader is referred to the following two textbooks: Jeffrey A. Timmons and Stephen Spinelli, *New Venture Creation*, 7th ed. (New York: McGraw-Hill/Irwin, 2007); and Michael J. Roberts, Howard H. Stevenson, William A. Sahlman, and Paul W. Marshall, *New Business Ventures and the Entrepreneur* (New York: McGraw-Hill/Irwin, 2006).

Chapter 15: Develop a Simple, Effective Business Plan

1. For further reading on business planning, the reader is referred to the following: William D. Bygrave and Andrew Zacharakis, *The Portable MBA in Entrepreneurship*, 4th ed. (Hoboken, NJ: John Wiley & Sons, 2005), pp. 107–139; Jeffrey A. Timmons and Stephen Spinelli, *New Venture Creation*, 7th ed. (New York: McGraw-Hill/Irwin, 2007); and David H. Bangs, *The Business Planning Guide:*

Creating a Plan for Success in Your Own Business (Denver, CO: Upstart Publishing, 1995).

2. Justin J. Camp, *Venture Capital Due Diligence: A Guide to Making Smart Investment Choices and Increasing Your Portfolio Returns* (Hoboken, NJ: John Wiley & Sons, 2002).

3. The Center for Competitive Success, "The Beading Café: Example of an Executive Summary." Copyright © Michael E. Gordon, 2000. Used with permission.

4. The Center for Competitive Success, "Your Executive Summary: A 10-Point Self Critique." Copyright © Michael E. Gordon, 2000. Used with permission.

Chapter 16: Become a Win-Win Negotiator

1. For further reading on negotiation, the following materials are recommended: Roger Fisher and William Ury, *Getting to Yes: Negotiating Agreement without Giving In* (Boston: Houghton Mifflin, 1981); Jane S. Flaherty and Peter B. Stark, *The Only Negotiating Guide You'll Ever Need: 101 Ways to Win Every Time in Any Situation* (New York: Broadway Books, 2003); Roger Dawson, *Secrets of Power Negotiating* (Franklin Lakes, NJ: The Career Press, 2001); Deborah M. Kolb and Judith Williams, *Breakthrough Bargaining* (Cambridge, MA: Harvard Business School Publishing, 2001), pp. 89–97.

2. Roger Fisher and William Ury, *Getting to Yes: Negotiating Agreement without Giving In* (Boston: Houghton Mifflin, 1981).

3. William Ury, *Getting Past No: Negotiating Your Way from Confrontation to Cooperation* (New York: Bantam Books, 1993).

4. The Center for Competitive Success, "When All Else Fails Think BABSON." Copyright © Michael E. Gordon, 2000. Used with permission.

Chapter 17: Raise Money

1. For further reading on raising capital, the reader is referred to the following: Bruce Blechman and Jay Conrad Levinson, *Guerrilla Financing: Alternative Techniques to Finance Any Small Business* (Boston: Houghton Mifflin, 1991); James Henderson, *Obtaining Venture Financing: A Guide for Entrepreneurs* (Boston: Lexington Books, 1988); Gerald A. Benjamin and Joel B. Margulis, *Angel Financing: How to Find and Invest in Private Equity* (New York: John Wiley & Sons, 2000); and David R. Evanson, *Where to Go When the Banks Say No: Alternatives for Financing Your Business* (Princeton, NJ: Bloomberg Press, 1998).

2. Bruce Blechman and Jay Conrad Levinson, *Guerrilla Financing: Alternative Techniques to Finance Any Small Business* (Boston: Houghton Mifflin, 1991).
3. Justin J. Camp, *Venture Capital Due Diligence: A Guide to Making Smart Investment Choices and Increasing Your Portfolio Returns* (Hoboken, NJ: John Wiley & Sons, 2002).

Chapter 18: Fixate on the Customer

1. Richard Whiteley and Diane Hessan, *Customer Centered Growth: Five Proven Strategies for Building Competitive Advantage* (New York: Addison-Wesley, 1996).

Chapter 19: Launch Your Venture!

1. Jay Conrad Levinson, *Guerrilla Marketing: Secrets for Making Big Profits from Your Small Business* (New York: Houghton Mifflin, 1998).
2. Beverly Inman Ebel, *Success Is a Decision of the Mind* (Hamilton, Queensland, Australia: Insight Publishing, 2004).

Chapter 20: Suffer Growing Pains Joyfully

1. Michael E. Porter, *Competitive Advantage: Creating and Sustaining Superior Performance* (New York: Free Press, 1998).
2. Neil C. Churchill and Virginia Lewis, "The Five Stages of Small Business Growth," in *The Entrepreneurial Venture*, ed. William A. Sahlman and Howard H. Stevenson (Boston: Harvard Business School Publications, Practice of Management Series, 1991), pp. 263–276; and discussions with Edward Marram, director of the Arthur M. Blank Center for Entrepreneurship, Babson College, regarding his research, teaching, and case materials on entrepreneurial growth.
3. Peter Schwartz, *Inevitable Surprises: Thinking Ahead in a Time of Turbulence* (New York: Gotham Books, 2003).
4. Thomas L. Friedman, *The World Is Flat: A Brief History of the Twenty-First Century* (New York: Farrar, Straus and Giroux, 2005).

INDEX

Due diligence, 156, 166, 192–193
Dunn and Bradstreet, 81

E

Early-stage funding, 189–191
Earnings before interest, taxes, depreciation, and amortization (EBITDA), 132
  as profit from operations (PFO), 140
eBay, 26, 102–104, 187
  Pierre Omidyar and, 87–88
Edison, Thomas, 17
Einstein, Albert, 194
Entrepreneur, 40
Entrepreneurial power skills, 4–13, 178
  act decisively, 12
  asses the present situation, 10–11
  behave with integrity, 12–13
  be unstoppable, 11
  brainstorm, 12, 25–27
  communicate effectively, 12
  go after bold visions, 10–11
    Power of Zero, 11
  make good decisions, 12
  mobilize powerful resources, 12
  negotiate firmly and "win winly," 11
  solve problems, 11–12

Entrepreneurial resources, 145–151
  financial, 150
  imagination, 151
  infrastructure, 151
  knowledge, 150–151
  physical, 149–150
  people, 146–149
    advisors, 148
    business service providers, 148–149
    company culture, 147–148
    family and friends, 149
    management team, 147
    partners, 147
    you, 147
Entrepreneurship, 7
  ability to learn and, 3, 10, 13
  actions and, 7–8
  brainstorming and, 25–27
  Donald Trump on, 1–3
  Gordon's CUSTOMER model, 28–35
  ideas and, 36–47
    fit and, 45–47
  mindset and, 7–8
  mobilizing resources and, 2, 144, 153, 206–208
  opportunity and, 22, 31–32, 36, 48–61
  as personal voyage, 8, 16
    life goals for, 9–10
      Michael Gordon's example of, 9–10
    obstacles during, 8, 15–24
      career risks, 21, 24
      doubt, 23–24

Learn the Trump Way to Market Your Business

Make no mistake: A Trump University marketing course can give you the knowledge and tools to accelerate the growth of your business — IF you're ready.

You will learn how to:

☐ Focus your business on the areas your customers care most about.

☐ Expand the scope of your business and acquire new customers.

☐ Maximize customer retention rate.

☐ Make your products/services irresistible to prospects.

☐ Develop an advertising message that works.

☐ And much more!

Trump University has a marketing course that's right for you, including:

☐ **Build a Profitable Marketing Plan:** Proven Marketing Strategies to Understand your Customer and Position your Product

☐ **Keep them Coming Back:** Customer Retention Strategies that Work Every Time

☐ **Accelerate your Business Growth:** Successful Marketing Strategies for New Products

☐ **Develop a *Trump Quality* Image:** How to Create First Rate Branding, Advertising and Public Relations

Each course is created by Don Sexton and features exclusive, cutting-edge content; experiential learning using simulations and realistic scenarios; interactive tools you can use in the real world; and comprehensive support from course facilitators.

Is a Trump University marketing course right for you?
There's really only one good way to find out.
Just visit **www.TrumpUniversity.com/LearnMarketing**

TRUMP
UNIVERSITY

www.TrumpUniversity.com